Gino's
VEG ITALIA!
The healthier way to eat Italian

GINO D'ACAMPO

Gino's VEG ITALIA!

The healthier way to eat Italian

GINO D'ACAMPO

HODDER &
STOUGHTON

I AM DEDICATING THIS BOOK
TO MY MOTHER ALBA,
OR AS I CALL HER:
THE VEGETABLE QUEEN.

CONTENTS

INTRODUCTION

Vegetables are a key element of Italian cuisine, particularly in the south of the country, yet in most Italian cookery books they play second fiddle to meat and fish dishes. That is why I really wanted to write this book – to celebrate vegetables and make them the star attraction rather than simply the supporting cast. But, just to be clear, although none of the recipes contain meat or fish this is not a 'vegetarian cookbook' as such. The recipes are for everyone, and I guarantee your family and friends will love them. If you are a strict vegetarian, you'll be able to make all the recipes in this book provided you use rennet-free equivalents of the cheeses.

The dishes I have chosen are full of flavour, easy to prepare, good for you and extremely satisfying. I have been making a lot of them regularly for many years, but some are new creations. They are not only impressive, but also extremely economical.

There is so much goodness in so many vegetables that they really can help our bodies to work better and stay healthier. They provide essential vitamins, minerals and fibre – all of which are needed for optimum health and well-being. Some are rich in iron, others in omega 3 and omega 6 or calcium. Many vegetables also contain carotenoids, which are believed to reduce the risk of developing certain diseases, including cancer.

With so many unexplained diseases around, I sometimes wonder whether many modern ailments might be attributable in part to the way we eat today – especially where processed foods are concerned. Although their packaging often claims they are fresh and healthy, they frequently contain chemicals that have been added to give them a longer shelf life. If you cook with fresh produce, you are more able to control what you consume – so let's go back to basics and enjoy what nature wanted us to eat!

For the best results in your cooking, I urge you to grow your own vegetables and herbs if at all possible. Even if you live in a tiny flat you can still grow a pot of basil, sage or rosemary on your windowsill, and if you have a small outdoor area – such as a balcony or patio – you can grow many vegetables in pots. It is honestly so worth it. In fact, I actually got the idea of writing this book because I started to grow my own. I had always grown herbs in London, but when I bought my house in Sardinia I built some very simple raised beds out of timber and this year have grown and harvested courgettes, peppers, aubergines, herbs, salad leaves and tomatoes as well as a range of fruits. No chemical fertilisers or pesticides – just sun and water, the way it's supposed to be, and I can honestly say I've never tasted fruit and vegetables quite like them. As well as having so much more flavour and being that much more nutritious, home-grown vegetables have given me enormous pleasure and satisfaction.

I am a great lover of meat and fish, but vegetables definitely deserve a book in their own right. If I haven't convinced you yet, just scan through these pages and look at the recipes on offer. As you can see from the photographs, the dishes look as incredible as they taste, yet all contain simple ingredients – and they're really easy to make. I have thoroughly enjoyed creating this book, and hope you enjoy the journey too. As always, I leave you with my promise – that my recipes are made with minimum effort, yet give maximum satisfaction.

Buon Appetito!

MY TOP 10 VEGETABLES

Here I have selected my favourite ten vegetables – the ones I cook with at least once a week. I would miss each of them enormously if they weren't part of my regular diet. You will notice that I haven't included onions and garlic, which are of course hugely important; I've concentrated on vegetables that feature in their own right rather than those used predominantly for flavouring. One that I haven't included, which I really did battle with, is the ubiquitous tomato. Tomatoes are one of the most popular fruits/vegetables in the world and are a key element of the Italian diet. They are extremely important to me, but I decided for my Top 10 to select ingredients that aren't used as frequently. My guilt, however, means I had to give them a mention!

ARTICHOKES

Globe artichokes have such a delectable flavour and are a real treat in our house. Generally, the ones in Italy (and there are several kinds) are more tender than those in Britain, so the whole vegetable can be eaten, either stewed, fried or even served raw with oil and lemon. However, in Britain I tend to use only the hearts, which are beautifully tender and delicious. Extracting the heart from a whole artichoke can be a lot of work, so I usually buy them ready-prepared. They are widely available in jars or tubs, marinated in oil and sometimes chargrilled, and are invaluable for using as an ingredient in cooking or popped into salads, giving you that elegant Mediterranean twist when you need it and saving you a lot of preparation time.

The artichoke is one of the oldest medicinal plants used for digestive and liver problems, and one artichoke contains approximately a quarter of the average adult's daily fibre requirements. It is packed with potassium, magnesium and folic acid, so is particularly good for pregnant women, and some studies show it even lowers cholesterol.

See Spaghetti with Artichokes, Radicchio, Peas and White Wine (page 102); Cavolo Nero, Rocket and Artichoke Tart with Provolone Cheese (page 150); Risotto Timbale with Butternut Squash, Artichokes and Aubergines (page 170); Lentils and Artichokes with Salsa Verde (page 239).

ASPARAGUS

The minute you start seeing these beautiful spears in your local grocers you know spring has arrived. There are green, white and even purple varieties, but green are the most commonly grown. Asparagus is a really classy vegetable that can look spectacular served as a starter or as a side dish.

Always buy asparagus in season (mid-spring to early summer) and try to source spears that have been locally grown and harvested as recently as possible. Probably more than any other vegetable, asparagus tastes best immediately after cutting.

To prepare asparagus, trim the woody base of the stalk (it can be snapped off if very fresh) and add the spears to salted boiling water or, even better, steam them, until just al dente. If overcooked, asparagus can become soggy and lose its flavour, its bright green

colour and its nutritious qualities. Fine asparagus cooks more evenly than larger spears. If using large spears, you will have to cook the stems longer than the tips.

Asparagus is full of nutrients, including folic acid, and can help protect against certain cancers and heart disease; it also boosts your immune system.

See Asparagus, Ricotta, Chilli and Parmesan Tartlets (page 43); Sunflower Bread Topped with Egg, Asparagus and Mayonnaise (page 53); Summer Vegetable and Asiago Cheese Frittata (page 73); Asparagus and Radicchio Risotto with Sage (page 166); Summer Vegetable Stew with Cheesy Dumplings (page 178).

AUBERGINES

Much loved in the Mediterranean, aubergines have a distinctive earthy flavour and lovely soft texture. They come in many shapes, colours and sizes, but whichever type you're buying the same rules apply: choose specimens with glossy, bright skin that feels firm to the touch and avoid any that are shrivelled or bruised.

I think many people are slightly wary of using aubergines as they have a reputation of being bitter and watery. Although it is traditional to salt them to extract the bitter juices, newer varieties are picked younger and are less bitter than they used to be, so salting is no longer necessary. However, salting does reduce the huge amount of oil they soak up during cooking. If you want to salt them, put chopped or sliced aubergines (depending on the recipe) in a colander, sprinkle over about 1 tablespoon of salt, then place a weight (such as a dish) on top to speed up the process. Finally, rinse and dry them before cooking.

Studies show that aubergines can control high blood cholesterol and their skin is full of vitamins and contains anthocyanins, which help to protect against cancer and other diseases.

See Grilled Aubergine Parcels Filled with Asiago, Tomatoes and Basil (page 32); Orecchiette with Spicy Roasted Vegetables (page 92); Aubergine Lasagne with Capers, Garlic and Parmesan (page 107); Cheesy Polenta with Spicy Roasted Aubergine Sauce (page 128); Baked Spinach Polenta with Vegetable Ragu (page 132); Risotto Timbale with Butternut Squash, Artichokes and Aubergines (page 170); Roasted Vegetable Ratatouille (page 183); Aubergine Parmigiana (page 187); Spicy Roasted Vegetable Couscous Salad (page 215); Aubergine and Courgette Gratin with Mozzarella (page 240); Roast Potatoes and Aubergines with Garlic and Lemon (page 242).

Broccoli is a firm favourite with my children and it's therefore served frequently in the D'Acampo household. It's such a versatile vegetable. When cooking for my children when they were babies, I added it to boiling pasta five minutes before the end of cooking time, then drained it and added butter and cheese. I also always include it in cauliflower cheese (it not only tastes great, but looks more colourful too) and I throw it into soups and stews or simply steam it. Every which way, it's a winner. Please don't overcook broccoli – you lose the texture and all the goodness it has to offer.

This vegetable is a great source of vitamins A and K, which really help those of you who have a vitamin D deficiency, as A and K vitamins keep the vitamin D metabolism in balance.

See Bruschetta with Three Toppings (page 49); Summer Vegetable and Asiago Cheese Frittata (page 73); Orecchiette with Spicy Roasted Vegetables (page 92); New Potato, Tenderstem Broccoli and Hazelnut Salad with Gorgonzola (page 229).

CARROTS

Every time I make a stew, soup or *soffritto* a carrot is added, so this vegetable had to be in my Top 10. The high vitamin A content really does help with eyesight, and this has to be the only vegetable that is actually more nutritious when cooked than when eaten raw.

The first cultivated carrots were purple, yet over the past few centuries bright orange carrots, developed in northern Europe, have become the norm. In recent years, there has been a movement to resurrect the old-style carrots (often called 'heritage carrots') and variety in shape and colour is re-emerging – some are purple, others white; some are small and plump, while others are long and spindly. They are full of flavour and well worth seeking out or growing yourself if you have the space. It's always worth buying organic carrots wherever possible, particularly if using baby carrots.

See Summer Vegetable Stew with Cheesy Dumplings (page 178); Pearl Barley and Curly Kale Stew with Sage (page 181); Roasted Root Vegetable Soup with Caramelised Onion Topping (page 197); The d'Acampo Family's Minestrone (page 200); Winter Vegetable and Spinach Soup (page 201); Traditional Italian Peasant's Soup (page 202); Pearl Barley, Fennel and Cannellini Bean Soup with Cheesy Panini (page 208); Warm Honeyed Parsnip, Carrot and Beetroot Salad with Horseradish Dressing (page 224).

CHICORY (INCLUDING RADICCHIO)

Chicory, including the red-leaved variety known as radicchio, is known for its distinctive bitter taste and is much loved in Italy. In Britain, where palates are less accustomed to the flavour, it is often grown in dark rooms to ensure a smoother taste. As a general rule, the darker the colour of the leaves, the more bitter the flavour.

White (also known as 'green') chicory and radicchio can be eaten raw or cooked (they become less bitter when cooked) and work well in salads, complementing sweeter-flavoured ingredients such as tomatoes, avocados, sweetcorn and tuna. I also enjoy chicory chargrilled and radicchio stirred into risottos.

Chicory contains inulin, which is a probiotic and therefore good for the digestive system. Some medical sources say that you should avoid chicory if you are pregnant or breastfeeding.

See Spaghetti with Artichokes, Radicchio, Peas and White Wine (page 102); Asparagus and Radicchio Risotto with Sage (page 166); Chargrilled Little Gem Lettuce, Chicory and Pea Salad (page 226).

COURGETTES

I eat courgettes (known in Italy as *zucchine*) at least two or three times a week, particularly when they are in season (from early summer to early autumn). There are so many ways to cook and enjoy them. As well as cooking them in the ways suggested in this book, you can simply fry them with some onion and add them to a creamy pasta sauce, or finely slice and grill them then marinate them in olive oil – or add them to your *soffritto*. If they're young they're delicious eaten raw, for instance in a salad.

When buying courgettes, select smaller specimens with soft skins; the larger, tougher-skinned ones will be turning into marrows. Consider growing your own – they are so easy to grow in pots on

a balcony or patio and are exquisite plucked from the plant when tiny. If frying courgettes, you may like to salt them as you do for aubergines, to extract excess water and reduce the amount of oil needed for cooking.

Courgettes are believed to have anti-cancer properties and they also play a role in promoting all-round cardiovascular health.

See Courgette Roll-ups Filled with Ricotta, Walnuts and Chargrilled Peppers (page 35); Courgette and Oozing Mozzarella Omelette (page 71); Courgette Fritters with Three Cheese and Herb Dip (page 78); Orecchiette with Spicy Roasted Vegetables (page 92); Cannelloni Filled with Courgettes, Ricotta and Provolone Cheese (page 108); Venetian-style Pasta Shells Stuffed with Courgettes and Sage (page 111); Baked Spinach Polenta with Vegetable Ragu (page 132); Pizza Topped with Four Cheeses, Courgette and Fresh Basil (page 139); Roasted Vegetable Pie with Lemon Zest and Fresh Rosemary (page 152); Courgette and Roasted Pepper Risotto with Provolone Cheese (page 164); Summer Vegetable Stew with Cheesy Dumplings (page 178); Roasted Vegetable Ratatouille (page 183); The D'Acampo Family's Minestrone (page 200); Traditional Italian Peasant's Soup (page 202); Spicy Roasted Vegetable Couscous Salad (page 215); Courgette Carpaccio with Borlotti Beans, Peppers and Capers (page 216); Baby Courgettes Marinated in Garlic and Herb Vinaigrette (page 235); Aubergine and Courgette Gratin with Mozzarella (page 240).

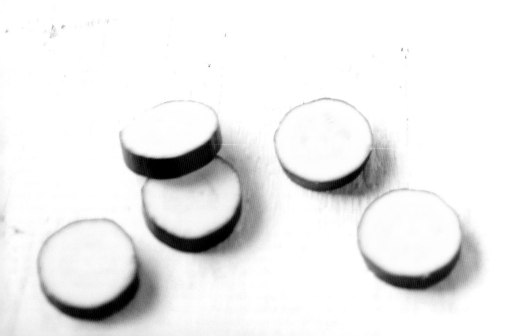

MUSHROOMS

In Italy we eat a lot of mushrooms. They tend to be wild mushrooms, picked in autumn, but we also use dried ceps, or porcini, which are widely available in Britain too. Not only do mushrooms taste fantastic and completely change the flavour of a dish when added, but they are also incredibly nutritious. They are a good source of iron, selenium and vitamin B and are also an excellent way to boost vitamin D levels.

Please do not pick wild mushrooms unless you really know what you're doing, as they can be lethal if you eat the wrong kind. Fortunately, an increasing range of wild and cultivated mushrooms is available in the shops nowadays. Do experiment with different varieties – each one has a distinct flavour and will really enhance your dish.

To prepare fresh mushrooms, just wipe them with a clean, damp cloth – they should be exposed to water as little as possible – then cut off the base of the stalks. Do not peel them. When using dried mushrooms, soak them in hot water for about 20 minutes before cooking to soften them.

A fascinating fact that I discovered when researching this book is that scientists studying the genetic material of fungi have discovered that mushrooms are closer to animals, including humans, than they are to plants. Amazing!

See Baked Penne in Puff Pastry with Leeks, Mushrooms and Mascarpone (page 112); Gnocchi with a Creamy Mushroom and Pea Sauce (page 122); Fried Polenta with Baked Cheesy Mushrooms and Parsley Butter (page 130); Risotto Dome with Mushrooms (page 168); Lentil and Mushroom 'Meatballs' with Herb Salsa (page 191).

PEPPERS

I love all kinds of peppers and they are a key element of the Mediterranean diet. They add colour, flavour and crunch to any dish. Many shapes, sizes and colours are available, and they can be packed with heat or sweetness, which makes them that bit sexier.

The most common type is the bell pepper, which is available in great vibrant colours, including red, orange, yellow and green. Red peppers tend to be sweeter than the green ones, while the orange and yellow varieties are more similar to the red kind. Red peppers are the most nutritious (11 times more beta-carotene and 1.5 times more vitamin C than a green pepper), mainly because they have been on the vine longer, but all varieties contain those fantastic vitamins and minerals that help our bodies function that much better.

When buying peppers, choose smooth, glossy, bright-coloured specimens and avoid any that are wrinkled or patchy. When preparing hot peppers (chillies), do be careful and wash your hands really well afterwards, or use gloves; the spice lingers on your fingers and can burn your skin and eyes. Deseed them (which includes removing the membrane as well as the seeds) if you don't want too much heat.

See Courgette Roll-ups Filled with Ricotta, Walnuts and Chargrilled Peppers (page 35); Bruschetta with Three Toppings (page 49); Frittata with Potatoes, Red Peppers and Mint (page 74); Orecchiette with Spicy Roasted Vegetables (page 92); Fusilli with Mascarpone and Yellow Pepper Sauce with Basil and Rocket (page 104); Pasta Salad with Spicy Black Olive Pesto (page 115); Saffron Polenta with Sweet Pepper, Olive and Caper Sauce (page 129); Pizza Tray with a Chargrilled Pepper, Olive and Caper Topping (page 140); Super-spicy Calzone with Sweet Peppers and Olives (page 147);

SPINACH

We love spinach in Italy, serving it as a side dish with other ingredients added and putting it into salads, pancakes, pasta, gnocchi and vegetable pies. Quite often, when spinach is used in dishes, particularly when added to a creamy sauce, the dish is called 'Florentine'. This is because Catherine de Medici (Italian noblewoman and wife of France's King Henry II) introduced spinach to the court of France to honour her Italian heritage and decided that any dish containing spinach should be named after her beloved home city of Florence.

When buying spinach, choose leaves that are brightly coloured and fresh looking. Wash in several changes of water, pick over the leaves, rejecting any that are withered, and discard tough stalks. If you're using frozen spinach, as some of these recipes suggest, do make sure you drain it well and squeeze out as much excess liquid as you can before cooking, as it can be very watery and can spoil the consistency of a dish.

This wonderful leaf is rich in vitamins and iron, but it does contain a high amount of oxalic acid, so for those who have kidney stones it is best to avoid over-consumption, particularly of raw spinach (light cooking does reduce the acid content). And the good news is that researchers have now found that the leaf membranes boost weight loss by 43 per cent, as they curb food cravings by 95 per cent. So it's delicious, healthy and also keeps you trim – win-win!

See Spinach and Bel Paese Filo Tart (page 36); Neapolitan Pasta Frittata (page 101); The Ultimate Pasta Bake with Five Cheeses, Peas and Spinach (page 105); Baked Gnocchi with Cannellini Beans, Spinach and Tomatoes (page 126); Baked Spinach Polenta with Vegetable Ragu (page 132); Pizza Cake with Semi-dried Tomatoes, Spinach and Goat's Cheese (page 144); Spinach, Rocket and Cheese Pie with a Hint of Chilli (page 153); Super-creamy Risotto with Prosecco, Nutmeg and Spinach (page 167); Winter Vegetable and Spinach Soup (page 201); Spinach and Chickpeas with Chilli and Garlic (page 236).

ANTIPASTI
and things to share

When I first mentioned to friends and family that I was writing a book celebrating vegetables quite a few of them expressed some concern over this chapter, assuming that Italians always start meals with cured meats or fish. They needn't have worried; there are so many vegetarian choices – in fact, I found it hard to select just eight!

In my family, we always start the meal with antipasti – whether it's just a taste of bruschetta before an informal supper or an impressive array of six to ten different dishes served to guests at a dinner party. I absolutely love this part of the meal – the sharing of good food with friends and family creates such a relaxed atmosphere and I can't tell you how many times people have said that they would be happy with just the antipasti.

Always remember, if you're serving antipasti at the start of the meal the idea is to stimulate the taste buds in preparation for the next course – not to spoil appetites. Plenty of variety is a good thing, but if your portions are too large your guests will fill up too soon. If you're serving just drinks, for instance at a cocktail party, you can be more generous.

The visual aspect of antipasti dishes is really important, so think about colour combinations and garnishes and how you can make the dishes look as attractive and tempting as possible. The appetite should be stimulated in the imagination first, then again after tasting, so take time and care to present the food beautifully.

The antipasti dishes I have selected are real showstoppers. Although I have included only eight in this chapter, you will find recipes elsewhere that are suited to serving before a main meal – for instance *arancini* (rice croquettes), salads and polenta – just adjust the portion sizes and quantities accordingly. And finally, remember to serve warm, rustic bread with your antipasti, in true Italian style.

Buffalo Mozzarella with Fresh
Tomato and Chilli Salsa

Grilled Aubergine Parcels Filled with
Asiago, Tomatoes and Basil

Borlotti Bean and Ricotta Pâté with
Garlic and Thyme

Courgette Roll-ups Filled with Ricotta,
Walnuts and Chargrilled Peppers

Spinach and Bel Paese Filo Tart

Fennel, Orange and Watercress
Salad with Thyme Vinaigrette

Grilled Avocado Stuffed with Tomatoes,
Spring Onions, Olives and Capers

Asparagus, Ricotta, Chilli and
Parmesan Tartlets

BUFFALO MOZZARELLA WITH FRESH TOMATO AND CHILLI SALSA

Mozzarella di Bufala con Salsa di Pomodori Piccanti

Originating in southern Italy, where fresh, creamy buffalo mozzarella is produced, this dish is simplicity at its best. Make it in summer, when tomatoes are at their juiciest and sweetest, and use a good-quality extra virgin olive oil to boost the flavour. Tomatoes are a rich source of vitamins, potassium and antioxidants, so this dish is full of goodness. Serve with some crusty rustic bread to mop up the delicious juices.

SERVES 6

3 x 125g balls of buffalo
   mozzarella cheese, drained
6 tablespoons shredded
   fresh basil

For the salsa
4 large fresh plum tomatoes,
   cut into 2cm chunks
½ red onion, peeled and
   finely chopped
1 fresh, medium-hot red chilli,
   deseeded and finely chopped
1 tablespoon sun-dried
   tomato paste
6 tablespoons chopped
   fresh oregano
Juice of 1 clementine
4 tablespoons extra virgin
   olive oil
Salt

1. To make the salsa, place the tomatoes, onion, chilli, sun-dried tomato paste and oregano in a medium bowl. Add the clementine juice and oil, season with a little salt and mix gently until everything is well coated with the dressing. Spoon the mixture into the centre of a large serving plate.

2. Cut each mozzarella ball into 6 slices and arrange all around the salsa. Scatter over the basil.

GRILLED AUBERGINE PARCELS FILLED WITH ASIAGO, TOMATOES AND BASIL

Fagottini di Melanzane Ripieni di Asiago, Pomodori e Basilico

Asiago cheese, which is made in the Veneto region in north-eastern Italy, has a slightly sweet, nutty flavour that complements aubergine perfectly. If you can't find Asiago, you could use 200g mozzarella instead. Cut the aubergines at the last minute to avoid discoloration. I have allowed for two parcels per person, making this quite a substantial first course. Serve with toasted ciabatta.

SERVES 4

2 large, long aubergines
125g Asiago cheese
2 large fresh plum tomatoes
16 fresh basil leaves,
    plus extra to garnish
2 tablespoons extra virgin olive oil
25g pistachios, roughly chopped,
    to garnish
Salt and freshly ground
    black pepper

For the dressing
4 tablespoons extra virgin olive oil
1 tablespoon balsamic vinegar
1 tablespoon sun-dried
    tomato paste
1 tablespoon freshly squeezed
    lemon juice
1/2 teaspoon dried chilli flakes

1. Bring a large pan of salted water to the boil. Using a long, sharp knife cut each aubergine lengthways into 8 thin slices. Discard the first and last slice.

2. Place the aubergines in the boiling water, bring back to the boil and cook for 2 minutes or until softened. Drain thoroughly then spread out on kitchen paper to dry.

3. Preheat the grill to medium high. Cut the Asiago into 8 slices and each tomato into 8 slices, discarding the first and last slice.

4. Now make the parcels: lay 2 slices of aubergine on top of each other to form a cross. Place a tomato slice in the centre of the cross and season with salt and pepper, then top the tomato with a basil leaf and a slice of Asiago. Add another basil leaf and tomato slice then season again. Bring up the ends of the aubergines, folding them up and over the filling to enclose it and form a parcel. Repeat until you have 8 parcels in total.

5. Brush both sides of the parcels with the oil, place on a baking sheet folded-side up and grill for 5 minutes, then turn and grill for a further 5 minutes or until golden. Meanwhile, whisk together all the dressing ingredients.

6. Arrange the grilled parcels, folded-side down, on a serving dish. Drizzle over the dressing and sprinkle over the pistachios and basil leaves. Serve hot or warm.

BORLOTTI BEAN AND RICOTTA PÂTÉ WITH GARLIC AND THYME

Pâté di Borlotti e Ricotta con Aglio e Timo

The borlotti bean is widely used in Italian cooking and has a lovely smooth, creamy texture and sweetish flavour that work well in this pâté. I often make this dish for summer barbecues and it always goes down a treat. Serve with crudités, bruschetta or breadsticks (see pages 57–58) and a bottle of chilled white wine.

SERVES 8

2 x 400g tins of borlotti beans,
    rinsed and drained
400g ricotta cheese
100g salted butter,
    cut into small cubes
1 large garlic clove, peeled
    and roughly chopped
Grated zest and juice of
    1 unwaxed lemon
3 tablespoons fresh thyme leaves
Handful (about 40g) of fresh
    flat-leaf parsley
1 tablespoon extra virgin olive oil
Salt and freshly ground
    black pepper

1. Place the beans, ricotta, butter, garlic and lemon zest and juice in a food processor and blitz until smooth. Season with salt and pepper, add the thyme and parsley and blitz again.

2. Spoon the mixture into a serving bowl or divide the pâté evenly between 8 individual ramekin dishes. Drizzle the oil over the top. Cover with cling film and chill in the fridge for 3 hours or until you are ready to serve.

COURGETTE ROLL-UPS FILLED WITH RICOTTA, WALNUTS AND CHARGRILLED PEPPERS

Rotolini di Zucchine Ripieni di Ricotta, Noci e Peperoni Grigliati

One of the great things about these little stuffed courgette rolls is that they don't require any cooking and can be prepared ahead. All that's needed is a bottle of chilled Italian white wine, some warm, crusty bread on the side and good friends to share them with. You can use hazelnuts instead of walnuts if you prefer.

SERVES 6

2 medium courgettes
6 tablespoons extra virgin olive oil
6 tablespoons balsamic vinegar
1 x 250g tub of ricotta cheese
1 tablespoon freshly squeezed
    lemon juice
50g walnuts, coarsely chopped
Small handful (about 25g) of
    shredded fresh basil
290g chargrilled peppers in a jar,
    drained and sliced into 24 pieces
Salt and freshly ground
    black pepper

1. Using a vegetable peeler, shave the courgettes lengthways into long, thin strips. You will need 24 strips in total.

2. Pour half the oil and half the vinegar into a large dish. Lay the courgette slices in the mixture, so that they do not overlap. Drizzle the remaining oil and vinegar over the top. Cover with cling film and put in the fridge to marinate for at least 30 minutes (they can be prepared several hours ahead).

3. Meanwhile, place the ricotta in a small bowl. Add the lemon juice, walnuts and basil. Season with salt and pepper and stir to combine.

4. Place 1 teaspoon of the ricotta mixture at one end of each courgette strip, lay a piece of pepper on top and roll up. Repeat until all the courgette strips, filling and peppers have been used. Arrange the rolls on a platter and serve.

SPINACH AND BEL PAESE FILO TART

Torta di Spinaci e Bel Paese in Sottile Pasta Sfoglia

Bel Paese is a mild, delicate cow's milk cheese originally produced in Milan. It can be used to replace mozzarella on a pizza, as it melts and oozes so beautifully; it's also a perfect match for spinach, as you'll discover if you make this recipe. This is an impressive tart to grace any table and always a winner.

SERVES 8

4 tablespoons sunflower oil
5 sheets filo pastry
500g frozen spinach,
    defrosted and drained
1 tablespoon olive oil
1 medium onion, peeled
    and finely chopped
140ml single cream
Large pinch of freshly
    grated nutmeg
125g Bel Paese cheese,
    cut into small chunks
Salt and freshly ground
    black pepper

1. Preheat the oven to 180°C/gas mark 4. Brush a 20cm loose-bottomed flan tin with a little of the sunflower oil.

2. Line the tin with the sheets of filo pastry, brushing the remaining sunflower oil between each layer and overlapping the sheets so they line the tin completely. Bake for 18 minutes or until the pastry turns a light golden brown and is cooked through.

3. Leave the pastry case to cool then remove from the tin and place on a baking sheet lined with baking parchment. Set aside. Squeeze out as much liquid from the spinach as you can.

4. Heat the olive oil in a medium saucepan over a medium heat. Add the onion and fry gently for about 3 minutes or until softened. Tip in the spinach and heat through for 3–5 minutes. Remove from the heat and stir in the cream, nutmeg, Bel Paese and some salt and pepper.

5. Carefully spoon the mixture into the cooled pastry case and bake for 15 minutes or until the filling has set. Serve the tart hot, warm or cold.

FENNEL, ORANGE AND WATERCRESS SALAD WITH THYME VINAIGRETTE

Insalata di Finocchi, Arance e Crescione con Vinaigrette al Timo

This zingy first-course salad takes only minutes to prepare yet is full of flavour and goodness. The peppery little leaves of the watercress are bursting with vitamins, minerals and antioxidants, making it one of our greatest natural superfoods, while the fennel and oranges are really rich in vitamin C. Try it with my Asparagus, Ricotta, Chilli and Parmesan Tartlets (see page 43).

SERVES 4

3 large oranges
Grated zest of 1 unwaxed lemon
1 shallot, peeled and grated
2 teaspoons runny honey
3 tablespoons fresh thyme leaves
7 tablespoons extra virgin olive oil
100g watercress, trimmed
1 large fennel bulb, cored and
    thinly sliced
Salt and freshly ground
    black pepper

1. First peel and segment 2 of the oranges. Using a sharp knife, cut off about 1–2cm from the top and bottom of the fruit to expose the flesh. Place the fruit on one of its flat ends and cut down to remove the skin and the white pith. Rotate and repeat, working your way around the fruit until the flesh is completely exposed.

2. Cut between the flesh and the white membrane to free the segments. Set the segments aside.

3. To make the vinaigrette, squeeze as much juice as you can from the remaining orange (you should have about 100ml). Put the orange juice in a bowl and add the lemon zest, shallot, honey and thyme then add the oil gradually. Season with a little salt and pepper. Whisk to combine.

4. Arrange the watercress on a large serving platter and scatter over the fennel, then the orange segments. Drizzle over the vinaigrette.

GRILLED AVOCADO STUFFED WITH TOMATOES, SPRING ONIONS, OLIVES AND CAPERS

Avocado Grigliato Ripieno di Pomodori, Cipollotti, Olive e Capperi

This dish is rather retro and I used to make it when I first came to London as a teenager. Make sure that the avocados are perfectly ripe and don't use buffalo mozzarella, as it will release too much milk during cooking. Grilling the avocado makes it softer and more velvety, but don't overcook or it will turn mushy. Serve with your favourite salad leaves.

SERVES 4

2 large ripe avocados,
   halved and stoned
1 tablespoon extra virgin olive oil
1 x 125g ball of mozzarella
   cheese, drained

For the filling
2 tablespoons extra virgin olive oil
1 fresh plum tomato, deseeded
   and cut into 1cm chunks
2 tablespoons sun-dried
   tomato paste
2 spring onions, roughly chopped
50g pitted green olives, drained
   and roughly chopped
1 tablespoon capers, drained
3 tablespoons freshly
   squeezed lemon juice
1 tablespoon sherry vinegar
2 teaspoons runny honey
Salt and freshly ground
   black pepper

1. Preheat the grill to medium high. Place the avocados on a baking sheet, cut-sides up, and brush the flesh with the oil. Grill for 5 minutes or until the flesh starts to brown. Set aside.

2. Combine the ingredients for the filling in a medium bowl. Divide the filling evenly between the avocado halves.

3. Cut the mozzarella into quarters, then cut each quarter into thirds. Top each stuffed avocado half with 3 mozzarella slices.

4. Place under the grill for 3 minutes or until the mozzarella starts to melt. Grind some black pepper over the top and serve immediately.

ASPARAGUS, RICOTTA, CHILLI AND PARMESAN TARTLETS

Crostatine Piccanti di Asparagi, Ricotta e Parmigiano

Asparagus is one of the great delicacies of the vegetable world, and my asparagus tartlets quite rightly make it centre of attention. It is cooked very briefly, then plunged into cold water to retain its texture and bright green colour. You can use pecorino cheese rather than Parmesan if you like a saltier flavour.

SERVES 4

200g fine asparagus spears, woody ends removed
1 x 320g sheet of shop-bought puff pastry (ready-rolled)
Plain flour for dusting
90g ricotta cheese
50g freshly grated Parmesan cheese
1 fresh, medium-hot red chilli, deseeded and finely chopped
8 tablespoons chopped fresh flat-leaf parsley
2 tablespoons chilli oil
Salt and white pepper

1. Preheat the oven to 200°C/gas mark 6. Bring a medium pan of salted water to the boil, add the asparagus, bring back to the boil and cook for 2 minutes. Drain and plunge immediately into cold water. Drain again then spread out on kitchen paper to dry.

2. Meanwhile, line a large baking sheet with baking parchment. Unroll the pastry onto a lightly floured work surface, cut into quarters using a long, sharp knife and lay the pastry rectangles on the lined baking sheet. Mark a border about 1cm in from the edge of the rectangles with the knife.

3. Place the ricotta, Parmesan, chilli, parsley, 1 tablespoon of the chilli oil and the salt and pepper in a medium bowl. Stir to combine.

4. Spoon the ricotta mixture over each pastry rectangle and spread to the inside edge of the border. Lay the asparagus on top. Brush the asparagus and pastry borders with the remaining oil.

5. Bake for 15–18 minutes or until the pastry is puffed up and golden. Serve immediately.

BREAD

and good things to put on it

I could probably live without potatoes and, if really pushed, possibly even rice. But bread – no way! You'll never find yourself sitting at my table – or any Italian's table – without a basket of bread on offer. And today, there are so many variations on the basic theme of flour, yeast and water; breads made with mixed grains, corn and soya mingle with countless others in the shops – all bringing us different tastes and textures.

In this chapter, I've chosen some of my firm favourites to share with you. Once you get the hang of how to make them, you can be as creative as you like; you can add olives, sun-dried tomatoes, nuts – whatever you fancy. In fact, more or less anything goes. In addition to the bread recipes (which include the Italian classics – *focaccia* and *ciabatta*), you have two recipes for *grissini* (breadsticks), which are great for snacks with drinks or dipping. There are also some suggestions for *panini*, which seem to keep on growing in popularity, and other Italian ways with delicious bread. When it's time for a quick lunch, you won't be disappointed!

A note on the bread recipes – it is difficult to say exactly how much liquid you should use for making bread dough, because the absorbency of flour can vary and it depends on which product you use. Remember, the dough should be sticky – if it is too dry the bread will be dry, so experiment and add a little more liquid as necessary.

Bruschetta with Three Toppings

Toasted Panini with Avocado, Taleggio,
Honey and Rocket

Sunflower Bread Topped with Egg,
Asparagus and Mayonnaise

Sun-dried Tomato Rolls Filled
with Fried Halloumi, Avocado and
Sweet Chilli Mayonnaise

Garlic and Fennel Seed Breadsticks
with Beetroot and Mint Dip

Salt and Pepper Breadsticks

Focaccia with Goat's Cheese and
Red Onion Marmalade

Focaccia with Pesto, Cherry Tomatoes
and Black Olives

Walnut and Raisin Ciabatta

BRUSCHETTA WITH THREE TOPPINGS

Bruschetta ai Tre Sapori

Bruschetta is served as a snack or antipasto in homes and bars all over Italy. Here I have come up with three quite different but equally delicious vegetable toppings. Serve together on a large platter or board (see photograph overleaf).

SERVES 4

1 large ciabatta loaf,
    cut into 12 slices
3 tablespoons extra
    virgin olive oil
1 garlic clove
Salt and freshly ground
    black pepper

For the bean topping
1 small red onion, peeled
    and finely sliced
Juice of 1 lemon
1 x 400g tin of cannellini beans,
    rinsed and drained
2 tablespoons extra virgin olive oil
1 tablespoon chopped fresh
    flat-leaf parsley

For the broccoli topping
100g Tenderstem broccoli
1 tablespoon olive oil
1 garlic clove, peeled and sliced
1/2 fresh, medium-hot red chilli,
    deseeded and finely sliced
20g Parmesan cheese shavings

For the pepper topping
2 tablespoons mascarpone cheese
1 tablespoon chopped fresh chives
100g chargrilled or roasted
    red peppers in a jar, drained
    and sliced

1. Preheat a ridged cast-iron chargrill pan over a high heat for 5–10 minutes. Brush the ciabatta on both sides with the oil. Place the slices in the pan in a single layer and chargrill for about 2 minutes each side or until golden brown. You will have to do this in batches. Rub one side of each slice with the garlic and set aside to cool (they can be made up to about 2 hours ahead).

2. To make the bean topping, place the onion in a small bowl, add half the lemon juice and a pinch of salt and leave to marinate for 10 minutes. Meanwhile, tip the beans into a medium bowl. Use the back of a fork to lightly crush the beans. Mix in the remaining lemon juice and the oil. Season with salt and pepper, add the parsley and stir again. Spoon the mixture onto 4 of the bruschetta (on the side rubbed with garlic) and spread evenly. Drain the onions, discarding the lemon juice, and place on top.

3. To make the broccoli topping, cook the broccoli in a medium saucepan of boiling, salted water for 2 minutes. Tip into a colander set over the sink and rinse for 1 minute under cold running water. Leave to drain. Meanwhile, heat the oil in a medium frying pan over a medium heat. Add the garlic and chilli, and when the garlic starts to sizzle add the broccoli. Stir-fry for 1 minute and season with salt. Spoon the broccoli onto 4 of the bruschetta and scatter over the Parmesan.

4. To make the pepper topping, mix the mascarpone with the chives in a small bowl and season with salt and pepper. Spread over the remaining 4 bruschetta and top with the red peppers.

TOASTED PANINI WITH AVOCADO, TALEGGIO, HONEY AND ROCKET

Panini Tostati con Avocado, Taleggio, Miele e Rucola

I love the combination of creamy cheese, runny honey, peppery rocket and smooth avocado in this recipe. As well as having a wonderful texture and flavour, avocados are so good for you – they are a rich source of protein, as well as packed with potassium and beneficial for cardiovascular health. Taleggio cheese melts beautifully, so is ideal for this recipe, but if you're unable to find it you could use mature Cheddar instead.

MAKES 2

2 ciabatta rolls
1–2 tablespoons olive oil
100g Taleggio cheese, rind
   removed and sliced
1 avocado, halved, stoned,
   peeled and sliced
1 teaspoon runny honey
Small handful (about 20g)
   of rocket leaves
Salt and freshly ground
   black pepper

1. Cut the rolls in half and brush the inside and outside with 1 tablespoon of the oil. Divide the Taleggio between the two bottom halves of the rolls and top with the avocado. Drizzle over the honey, add the rocket and season with salt and pepper. Cover with the top halves of the rolls.

2. If you have a panini toaster, cook for 2–3 minutes or until crispy and the cheese has started to melt. If not, heat 1 tablespoon of the oil in a frying pan over a medium heat and fry carefully on both sides, pressing down slightly with a fish slice as it cooks. Serve the panini immediately while warm and gooey.

SUNFLOWER BREAD TOPPED WITH EGG, ASPARAGUS AND MAYONNAISE

Pane ai Semi di Girasole Guarnito di Uova, Asparagi e Maionese

This delicious loaf is made with a mixture of wholemeal and white flour and contains sunflower seeds for added texture and flavour. It makes the most amazing posh open-faced egg and asparagus sandwich, which is my favourite thing to do with it.

**MAKES 1 LOAF AND
2 SANDWICHES**

225g strong white flour,
   plus extra for dusting
100g wholemeal flour
1x 7g sachet fast-action
   (easy blend) dried yeast
1 teaspoon salt
2 tablespoons extra virgin olive
   oil, plus extra for greasing
2 tablespoons sunflower seeds

For the topping
3 medium eggs
100g fine asparagus spears,
   woody ends removed
1 teaspoon olive oil
3 tablespoons mayonnaise
Grated zest of 1/2 lemon
1 teaspoon finely chopped
   fresh tarragon
Small punnet of cress
Salt and freshly ground
   black pepper

1. To make the loaf, place the flours in a large bowl. Add the yeast to one side of the bowl and the salt to the other. Make a well in the centre, add the oil and gradually pour in 220ml warm water, mixing together using the handle of a wooden spoon.

2. Knead the dough on a lightly oiled surface for about 8 minutes or until smooth. Shape into a round and place in a large, oiled bowl. Cover with cling film and leave in a warm place for about 1 hour or until doubled in size. Brush a large baking sheet with a little oil and set aside.

3. Turn out the dough onto an oiled surface, knead just 3 or 4 times then knead in the sunflower seeds. Shape into an oval and place on the oiled baking sheet. Cover with a tea towel and leave to rise again for about 40 minutes or until doubled in size. Meanwhile, preheat the oven to 200°C/gas mark 6. Bake the loaf for 30–35 minutes or until golden brown. Transfer to a wire rack to cool.

4. To make the topping, cook the eggs in a pan of simmering, salted water for 4 minutes, then add the asparagus and cook for a further 3 minutes. Drain the eggs and asparagus then place the eggs under cold running water for 2 minutes. Place the hot asparagus on a plate and drizzle with the oil. Season well and toss together. Set to one side to cool slightly. Peel and slice the cooled eggs and set aside. Combine the mayonnaise, lemon zest and tarragon in a small bowl and season.

5. Cut two thick slices of the sunflower bread and spread with some of the lemon and tarragon mayonnaise. Lay the sliced eggs on top, then the asparagus, then add another spoonful of the mayonnaise. Scatter over some cress with a few grindings of black pepper.

SUN-DRIED TOMATO ROLLS FILLED WITH FRIED HALLOUMI, AVOCADO AND SWEET CHILLI MAYONNAISE

Panini ai Pomodori Secchi, Imbottiti di Halloumi Fritto, Avocado e Maionese alla Salsa Dolce di Peperoncino

Sun-dried tomatoes have an intense, concentrated flavour and rich colour. Here I added them, together with oregano, to ordinary bread dough to make delicious aromatic rolls that complement the filling perfectly.

MAKES 8 ROLLS AND FILLING FOR 2 ROLLS

150ml warm, full-fat milk
1 x 7g sachet fast-action (easy blend) dried yeast
500g strong white flour, plus extra for dusting
1 teaspoon salt
100g salted butter, melted and cooled
100g sun-dried tomatoes in oil, drained, dried and chopped
1 teaspoon dried oregano

For the filling
1 tablespoon mayonnaise
1 teaspoon sweet chilli sauce
1 avocado, halved, stoned and peeled
2 spring onions, finely chopped
Juice of 1/2 lime
1 tablespoon olive oil
Pinch of sweet smoked paprika
150g halloumi cheese, cut into 4 slices
Handful of salad leaves
Salt and white pepper

1. To make the rolls, put the warm milk and 100ml warm water in a jug, add the yeast and stir until dissolved. Place the flour and salt in a large bowl and mix well. Make a well in the centre and add the milk mixture and melted, cooled butter. Mix together using the handle of a wooden spoon.

2. Knead the dough on a lightly floured surface for about 8 minutes until smooth. Shape into a round and place in an oiled bowl. Cover with cling film and leave in a warm place for about 2 hours until doubled in size. Dust 2 baking sheets with flour and set aside.

3. Turn out the dough onto a lightly floured surface, knead 3 or 4 times then knead in the sun-dried tomatoes and oregano. Divide into 8 equal-sized pieces and shape into balls. Place the balls well apart on the floured baking sheets. Dust the tops with flour and cover with a tea towel. Leave in a warm place for about 1 hour or until doubled in size. Preheat the oven to 190°C/gas mark 5. Bake for 28 minutes or until golden. Transfer to a wire rack to cool.

4. To make the filling, mix together the mayonnaise and sweet chilli sauce in a small bowl and set aside. Place the avocado in another bowl and mash with the back of a fork. Stir in the spring onions and lime juice, season and set aside. Heat the oil in a small frying pan over a high heat. Sprinkle the paprika over the halloumi and fry for 1 minute each side or until starting to turn golden.

5. Cut 2 rolls in half. Spread the mayonnaise mixture on the top halves and avocado mixture on the bottom halves. Lay the halloumi on top of the avocado, then some salad leaves. Cover with the top halves and eat straightaway.

GARLIC AND FENNEL SEED BREADSTICKS WITH BEETROOT AND MINT DIP

Grissini all' Aglio e Semi di Finocchio con Salsa di Rapa Rossa e Menta

Grissini are crunchy little breadsticks that are perfect for serving with pre-dinner drinks or as a snack. These garlic and fennel seed grissini are great served with the beetroot and mint dip described here (see photograph overleaf). However, you can serve them with any dip or just enjoy them on their own.

MAKES 20

400g strong white flour,
    plus extra for dusting
1 x 7g sachet fast-action
    (easy blend) dried yeast
2 teaspoons salt
3 tablespoons extra virgin olive
    oil, plus extra for greasing
50g finely grated Parmesan cheese
1 tablespoon fennel seeds, crushed
2 garlic cloves, peeled and
    finely chopped
Fine semolina for dusting
    (optional)

For the dip
250g cooked beetroot, halved
1 teaspoon honey
Juice of ½ lemon
15 fresh mint leaves
3 tablespoons crème fraîche
Salt and freshly ground
    black pepper

1. Place the flour in a large bowl. Add the yeast to one side of the bowl and the salt to the other. Make a well in the centre, pour in the oil and 250ml warm water and mix together using the handle of a wooden spoon. Gradually add another 100ml warm water, stirring as you go.

2. Knead the dough on a lightly floured surface for about 8 minutes or until it stretches easily without breaking. Sprinkle over the Parmesan, fennel and garlic, and knead again until well combined. Shape into a round and place in a large, oiled bowl. Cover with cling film and leave in a warm place for about 1 hour or until doubled in size.

3. Preheat the oven to 180°C/gas mark 4. Line 2 baking sheets with baking parchment and dust the work surface with plenty of flour and semolina, if using (it gives the breadsticks added crunch).

4. Turn out the dough onto a lightly floured surface, handling it carefully to retain as much air as possible (it will be quite wet at this stage). Stretch it out with your hands into a rectangle then cut into 20 strips. Take each strip and roll it on the floured surface to make a 20cm-long, thin sausage shape. Transfer to the lined baking sheets, spacing them well apart.

5. Bake for 18–20 minutes or until golden brown. Transfer to a wire rack to cool.

6. Meanwhile, make the dip. Place the beetroot, honey, lemon juice and mint in a food processor and blend until smooth. Add the crème fraîche, season and blend for 10 seconds until just incorporated. Put in a bowl, grind over some pepper and serve with the breadsticks.

SALT AND PEPPER BREADSTICKS

Grissini al Pepe e Sale

These simple salt and pepper grissini are delicious served with Beetroot and Mint Dip (see page 57) or Borlotti Bean and Ricotta Pâté with Garlic and Thyme (see page 33). I have given quantities for 20 breadsticks here, but if you have a party coming up you can easily make a double batch and store them in an airtight container for up to a week – giving you one less job to do on party day.

MAKES 20

400g strong white flour,
    plus extra for dusting
1 x 7g sachet fast-action
    (easy blend) dried yeast
2 teaspoons salt
3 tablespoons extra virgin olive
    oil, plus extra for greasing
Fine semolina for dusting
    (optional)
1 egg white, beaten with
    1 tablespoon water
1 tablespoon sea salt flakes
1 tablespoon coarsely ground
    black pepper

1. Place the flour in a large bowl. Add the yeast to one side of the bowl and the salt to the other. Make a well in the centre, pour in the oil and 250ml warm water and mix together using the handle of a wooden spoon. Gradually add another 100ml warm water, stirring as you go.

2. Knead the dough on a lightly floured surface for about 8 minutes or until it stretches easily without breaking. Shape the dough into a round and place in a large, oiled bowl. Cover with cling film and leave in a warm place for about 1 hour or until doubled in size.

3. Preheat the oven to 220°C/gas mark 7. Line 2 baking sheets with baking parchment and dust the work surface with plenty of flour and semolina, if using.

4. Turn out the dough onto a lightly floured surface, handling it carefully so that you keep as much air as possible in the dough (it will be quite wet at this stage). Stretch it out with your hands into a rectangle then cut into 20 strips. Take each strip and roll it on the floured surface to make a 20cm-long, thin sausage shape. Transfer to the lined baking sheets, spacing them well apart.

5. Gently brush the tops of each breadstick with a little egg white mixture then sprinkle with the sea salt and pepper. Bake for 12–15 minutes or until golden brown. Transfer to a wire rack to cool.

FOCACCIA WITH GOAT'S CHEESE AND RED ONION MARMALADE

Focaccia al Formaggio di Capra e Marmellata di Cipolle Rosse

With its dimpled surface, focaccia is unlike any other type of bread. It can be served as a main meal with salad, or as an antipasto with drinks. The quantities given in this recipe for the red onion marmalade will make more than you need for the focaccia, so just reserve 6 tablespoons, spoon the rest into a sterilised jar and store in the fridge until needed. If you don't have time to make onion marmalade, just buy it instead.

SERVES 8–10

500g strong white flour,
   plus extra for dusting
1 x 7g sachet fast-action
   (easy blend) dried yeast
2 teaspoons salt
6 tablespoons extra virgin olive
   oil, plus extra for greasing
100g soft goat's cheese
3 tablespoons fresh
   rosemary leaves
Large pinch of sea salt flakes

For the onion marmalade
25g salted butter
300g red onions, peeled and sliced
50g caster sugar
100ml red wine
2 tablespoons balsamic vinegar
Salt and white pepper

1. First make the onion marmalade. Melt the butter in a medium saucepan over a low heat. Add the onions, sugar, salt and pepper and cook gently for 30 minutes or until the onions are soft, stirring occasionally. Add the wine and vinegar and cook for a further 30 minutes or until thickened and the onions have caramelised. Leave to cool.

2. Place the flour in a large bowl. Add the yeast to one side of the bowl and the salt to the other. Make a well in the centre and add 3 tablespoons of the oil then gradually pour in 300ml warm water and mix together using the handle of a wooden spoon.

3. Knead the dough on a lightly floured surface for about 10 minutes or until smooth and elastic, adding a little more flour if it's really sticky. Shape the dough into a round and place in a large, oiled bowl. Cover with cling film and leave in a warm place for 1 hour or until doubled in size. Brush a large baking sheet with a little oil and set aside.

4. Turn out the dough onto a lightly floured surface, knead 3 or 4 times and transfer to the oiled baking sheet. Using your fingertips, gently push the dough to a rectangle about 30 x 24cm and 2–3cm thick. Brush with 1 tablespoon of oil, cover lightly with a tea towel and leave to rise for a further 40 minutes or until doubled in size. Meanwhile, preheat the oven to 200°C/gas mark 6.

5. Remove the tea towel and press your fingertips into the dough to create indentations. Drizzle over another tablespoon of the oil, dot with 6 tablespoons of the onion marmalade, then scatter over the goat's cheese, rosemary and sea salt. Brush with the remaining tablespoon of oil. Bake for 20 minutes or until golden brown. Transfer to a wire rack to cool slightly. Serve warm.

FOCACCIA WITH PESTO, CHERRY TOMATOES AND BLACK OLIVES

Focaccia al Pesto, Pomodorini e Olive Nere

Focaccia is particularly associated with the region of Liguria, in north-western Italy, where there are numerous variations on the theme – from plain to topped or stuffed focaccia. Pesto is also a speciality of the region, and when combined with fresh cherry tomatoes and black olives it makes the perfect partner for focaccia (see photograph overleaf).

SERVES 8

500g strong white flour, plus extra for dusting
1 x 7g sachet fast-action (easy blend) dried yeast
2 teaspoons salt
4 tablespoons extra virgin olive oil, plus extra for greasing

For the topping
2 tablespoons extra virgin olive oil
150g cherry tomatoes
100g pitted Kalamata olives, drained
Large pinch of sea salt flakes
3 tablespoons shop-bought pesto

1. Place the flour in a large bowl. Add the yeast to one side of the bowl and the salt to the other. Make a well in the centre and add 3 tablespoons of the oil then gradually pour in 300ml warm water and mix together using the handle of a wooden spoon.

2. Knead the dough on a lightly floured surface for about 10 minutes or until smooth and elastic, adding a little more flour if it's really sticky. Shape the dough into a round and place in a large, oiled bowl. Cover with cling film and leave in a warm place for 1 hour or until doubled in size. Brush a large baking sheet with a little oil and set aside.

3. Turn out the dough onto a lightly floured surface, knead just 3 or 4 times to knock out the air and transfer to the oiled baking sheet. Using your fingertips, gently push the dough to a rectangle about 30 x 24cm and 2–3cm thick. Brush with the remaining tablespoon of oil, cover lightly with a tea towel and leave to rise for a further 40 minutes or until doubled in size. Meanwhile, preheat the oven to 200°C/gas mark 6.

4. Remove the tea towel and press your fingertips into the dough to create indentations. Drizzle with most of the oil for the topping. Press the tomatoes into the indentations and scatter over the olives and the sea salt. Brush with the remaining oil. Bake for 20 minutes or until golden brown. Gently dot the top with the pesto and transfer to a wire rack to cool slightly. Serve warm.

WALNUT AND RAISIN CIABATTA

Ciabatta con Noci e Uvetta

Ciabatta means 'slipper' in Italian, and if you look at the shape you can see why. In Italy we usually serve ciabatta with antipasti, but this sweet, nutty version is perfect at other times too; my sons often like to eat it for breakfast with chocolate spread. Note that the 'starter' (or biga) *must be made the day before baking and left to rest overnight. Make sure you don't rush this stage, as resting will improve the flavour and texture of your ciabatta.*

MAKES 4 SMALL LOAVES

10g fresh yeast
450g strong white flour,
    plus extra for dusting
1 teaspoon salt
50ml extra virgin olive oil,
    plus extra for brushing
50g walnuts, roughly chopped
50g raisins

For the starter
5g fresh yeast
350g strong white flour
olive oil, for greasing

1. To make the starter, place the yeast and 180ml warm water in a large bowl. When the yeast has dissolved, add the flour and stir to combine for 5 minutes to form a rough dough. Grease the inside of another large bowl with a little oil and put in the dough. Cover with cling film and leave overnight, away from draughts.

2. The following day, place the yeast and 340ml warm water in a large bowl. When the yeast has dissolved, add the flour and the starter. Add the salt and pour over the olive oil. Mix until well combined.

3. Knead the dough on a lightly floured surface for about 10 minutes or until smooth. Place the dough in a large, oiled rectangular container, cover with cling film and leave to rise in a warm place for 2 hours or until doubled in size.

4. Turn out the dough onto a floured surface and sprinkle over a little flour. Gently press down with your fingers to flatten the rectangle to about 2cm thick then cut the dough into 4 equal-sized strips and scatter the walnuts and raisins over each strip.

5. Take one strip of dough, fold one short side of it into the middle, then bring the other side over to meet it. Press down to seal. Finally, fold in half lengthways and press to seal the edges to create a long shape. Repeat this process with the remaining strips of dough.

6. Cover a flat tray with a tea towel and sprinkle it with flour. Place the 4 folded loaves on the tea towel, cover with another tea towel and leave to rest in a warm place for 40 minutes or until doubled in size. Preheat the oven to 220°C/gas mark 6. Brush 2 baking sheets with a little oil.

7. Place the loaves on the prepared baking sheets, 2 per sheet, spaced apart and with the folded sides down. Gently stretch the dough lengthways to create the characteristic 'slipper' shape.

8. Spray the inside of the oven with water or splash a little water using your fingertips. Bake the loaves for 22 minutes or until golden brown. Transfer to a wire rack to cool slightly. Serve warm.

EGGS

As far as I'm concerned, eggs are the ultimate convenience food; they're quick and simple to prepare in all manner of ways – and they're full of goodness. Eggs are so versatile and can play such an important part at every mealtime – breakfast, lunch and dinner – that I felt I ought to dedicate an entire section to them.

Although many people keep eggs in the fridge to make them last longer, it's much better to store them at room temperature. Either way, make sure they are not chilled when you use them. Another tip: don't store them close to really pungent foods as their flavour can become tainted. And observe their use-by date – not only for safety reasons, but because stale eggs have flat yolks and watery whites, which will spoil the taste and texture of your dish.

In this chapter I've included a range of different types of egg dishes that work well with vegetables – omelettes and frittatas, of course, but also vegetable fritters, potato rösti topped with a poached egg, a lovely fennel and leek tart and vegetable-stuffed pancakes. Cold frittata is a personal favourite, as that's the dish I normally have as a packed lunch on my boat when I go fishing. It makes my day even when I don't catch anything and is a winner every time.

Courgette and Oozing Mozzarella Omelette

Summer Vegetable and Asiago
Cheese Frittata

Frittata with Potatoes, Red Peppers
and Mint

Three Cheese Soufflé Omelette

Cauliflower Fritters with Roasted
Garlic and Chilli Mayonnaise

Courgette Fritters with Three Cheese
and Herb Dip

Pancakes with Jerusalem Artichoke,
Leek and Cheese Filling

Potato Rösti and Poached Egg with
Fresh Herb Sauce

Fennel and Leek Tart with Pecorino Cheese

COURGETTE AND OOZING MOZZARELLA OMELETTE

Omelette con Zucchine e Mozzarella Fondente

Omelettes are versatile, quick to prepare and make a trusty standby dish for breakfast, lunch or supper. Courgettes are the perfect partner for eggs, with their delicate-tasting flesh and soft, creamy texture – particularly when grated, as in this recipe. They also combine beautifully with the melted mozzarella. Serve with warm, crusty bread.

SERVES 1

1 courgette, about 120g, grated
3 large eggs, lightly beaten
5g salted butter
2 tablespoons olive oil
1 x 125g ball of mozzarella cheese, drained and roughly chopped
1 tablespoon chopped fresh oregano
Salt and freshly ground black pepper

1. Place the courgette in a medium bowl with the beaten eggs. Season with salt and pepper and set aside.

2. Heat the butter and oil in a 20cm non-stick omelette pan or frying pan over a medium-high heat until the butter bubbles and foams. Pour in the egg and courgette mixture and tilt the pan to spread the mixture evenly over the bottom. Reduce the heat and cook for 5 minutes, without stirring.

3. When the omelette starts to set, scatter over the mozzarella. Continue to cook until the egg mixture has almost set.

4. Remove from the heat and leave to rest for 1 minute then sprinkle over the oregano. Fold the omelette in half using a fish slice and carefully slide onto a plate.

SUMMER VEGETABLE AND ASIAGO CHEESE FRITTATA

Frittatona d'Estate con Asiago

Containing several different green vegetables as well as new potatoes and cheese, this frittata is flavoursome, nutritious and substantial. It is best served hot, with the Asiago cheese oozing, but don't throw away any leftovers as it can also be eaten cold. If you can't find Asiago, use Brie instead. Serve with a crisp green salad.

SERVES 6

400g baby new potatoes,
   scrubbed and sliced into
   rounds 5mm thick
100g fine asparagus spears,
   woody ends removed and
   cut into 3cm lengths
100g broccoli, cut into
   small florets
100g frozen peas, defrosted
2 tablespoons olive oil
100g spring onions, chopped
2 tablespoons chopped
   fresh chives
3 tablespoons chopped
   fresh flat-leaf parsley
6 large eggs, lightly beaten
100g Asiago cheese,
   cut into small pieces
Salt and freshly ground
   black pepper

1. Put the potatoes in a large pan of boiling, salted water and bring back to the boil. Add the asparagus, broccoli and peas and cook for 4 minutes or until all the vegetables are just tender. Drain well and set aside.

2. Heat the oil in a 24cm heavy-based, non-stick frying pan over a medium heat. Add the spring onions and fry gently for 5 minutes, stirring occasionally. Add the drained vegetables and the herbs and fry for 2 minutes. Preheat the grill to medium high.

3. Season the beaten eggs with salt and pepper and pour them over the vegetables. Tilt the pan so the eggs cover the bottom of the pan evenly, reduce the heat slightly and cook for 8 minutes without stirring. Remove from the heat and scatter over the Asiago. Place the pan under the hot grill for about 6 minutes or until set and golden brown.

4. Remove from the grill and leave to rest in the pan for 5 minutes then turn onto a serving plate. Cut into wedges to serve.

FRITTATA WITH POTATOES, RED PEPPERS AND MINT

Frittata con Patate, Peperoni Rossi e Menta

A frittata is an Italian egg-based dish that is basically like a quiche but without the pastry casing. It's chunky and delicious and can include all kinds of ingredients, including meat, cheese, vegetables or even pasta (see page 101). This frittata can be served hot or cold and is the perfect dish to prepare ahead. Serve with a salad on the side.

SERVES 4

450g baby new potatoes,
  scrubbed
4 tablespoons olive oil
1 large onion, peeled and
  roughly chopped
2 red peppers, deseeded and
  roughly chopped
7 medium eggs, lightly beaten
6 tablespoons chopped fresh mint
Salt and freshly ground
  black pepper

1. Put the potatoes in a large pan of boiling, salted water, bring back to the boil and simmer gently for about 10–12 minutes or until just tender. Drain, halve and set aside.

2. Heat the oil in a 24cm heavy-based, non-stick frying pan over a medium heat. Add the onion, peppers and potatoes and fry gently for 15 minutes, stirring occasionally. Preheat the grill to a medium setting.

3. Season the beaten eggs with salt and pepper, add the mint and pour them over the potato mixture. Tilt the pan so the eggs cover the bottom of the pan evenly, reduce the heat slightly and cook for 6 minutes without stirring. Place under the hot grill for about 3 minutes until set and golden brown.

4. Remove from the grill and leave to rest in the pan for 5 minutes then turn onto a serving plate. Let cool completely then cut into wedges to serve.

THREE CHEESE SOUFFLÉ OMELETTE

Omelette Soufflé ai Tre Formaggi

The most impressive-looking of all omelettes is the soufflé omelette. Containing whisked egg whites, it is particularly light and fluffy and puffs up gloriously in the pan. I used Taleggio cheese in this recipe, because it's rich and creamy and melts easily, but if it's unavailable use grated mature Cheddar instead. Serve with a mixed salad or chips.

SERVES 2

4 large eggs, separated
50g mascarpone cheese
25g freshly grated Parmesan cheese
5g salted butter
1 tablespoon olive oil
25g Taleggio cheese, rind removed and cut into small cubes
Freshly ground black pepper

1. Put the egg whites in a medium bowl and whisk, ideally using an electric hand whisk, until very stiff. In another large bowl combine the mascarpone, Parmesan, egg yolks and pepper. Gently fold in the egg whites using a metal spoon, taking care not to knock out all the air bubbles.

2. Heat the butter and oil in a 24cm heavy-based, non-stick frying pan over a medium heat until the butter bubbles and foams. Pour in the egg and cheese mixture and tilt the pan to evenly distribute the mixture. Cook for 8 minutes, without stirring, until the sides have set.

3. Scatter the Taleggio over one half of the omelette. Continue to cook for a further 3 minutes. Fold the omelette in half using a fish slice and slide onto a flat serving plate. Leave to rest for 2 minutes.

CAULIFLOWER FRITTERS WITH ROASTED GARLIC AND CHILLI MAYONNAISE

Frittelle di Cavolfiore con Maionese all'Aglio Arrostito e Peperoncino

Italians love fritters, which are basically vegetables that are coated in batter and fried. My mum always used to make them for my sister Marcella and me when we got home from school every Friday; for us, it signalled the start of the weekend. You can serve these cauliflower fritters with drinks, or for a snack or light lunch. It's worth making your own mayonnaise if you have the time, but if not buy a good-quality brand and simply add garlic and chilli powder.

SERVES 4

¼ large cauliflower, about 130g, broken into very small florets
150g self-raising flour
2 medium eggs, lightly beaten
40g freshly grated Parmesan cheese
3 tablespoons chopped fresh flat-leaf parsley
60ml vegetable oil
Freshly ground black pepper

For the mayonnaise
½ head of garlic
1 large egg yolk
½ tablespoon sherry vinegar
¼ teaspoon salt
¼ teaspoon chilli powder
100ml vegetable oil

1. First make the mayonnaise. Preheat the oven to 180°C/gas mark 4. Wrap the garlic in foil and roast for 1 hour. Leave to cool. Unwrap the garlic and, over a medium bowl, squeeze the softened cloves out of their skins by pinching one end so the flesh pops out of its skin at the other. Using the back of a fork, mash the cloves to a paste.

2. Tip the egg yolk into the bowl with the garlic and whisk. Add the vinegar, salt and chilli powder then add the oil gradually, one drop at a time, whisking continually until thickened (this stage will take about 15 minutes, and it's important to not rush, otherwise the mayonnaise will split). Cover with cling film and chill until needed.

3. For the fritters, bring a medium saucepan of salted water to the boil, drop in the cauliflower and simmer for 5 minutes or until just tender. Drain and set aside.

4. Place the flour in a medium bowl. Make a well in the centre and add the beaten eggs. Add 7 tablespoons of cold water and whisk gently. Add the Parmesan, parsley and some pepper, stir, then add the cauliflower. Stir well to coat the cauliflower in the mixture.

5. Heat the oil in a 24cm heavy-based frying pan over a medium heat until very hot. To test the temperature, add a drop of the mixture; it will sizzle when the oil is hot enough for frying.

6. Spoon the cauliflower mixture into the hot oil, 1 tablespoon at a time and so the pieces are not touching (it should make 8 fritters). Fry without moving for 3 minutes, turn and continue to fry for a further 3 minutes or until golden and crispy all over. Remove with a slotted spoon and drain on kitchen paper. Serve with the mayonnaise.

COURGETTE FRITTERS WITH THREE CHEESE AND HERB DIP

Frittelle di Zucchine con Salsa alle Erbe e Tre Formaggi

Courgettes are among the most popular vegetables used for fritters. In fact, in Italy we even fry the courgette flowers. Courgette fritters are light, delicate and tasty on their own, but when accompanied by this cheesy, herby dip they are out of this world.

SERVES 5

1 large courgette,
    about 200g, grated
1 teaspoon salt, plus extra
    for seasoning
50g plain flour
1 large egg, beaten
100g ricotta cheese
2 garlic cloves, crushed
½ teaspoon chilli powder
3 tablespoons shredded
    fresh basil
3 tablespoons chopped
    fresh flat-leaf parsley
400ml vegetable oil

For the dip
50g ricotta cheese
50g mascarpone cheese
10g pecorino cheese,
    freshly grated
1 tablespoon freshly squeezed
    lemon juice
3 tablespoons chopped fresh dill
3 tablespoons chopped
    fresh oregano
Salt and white pepper

1. Place the courgette in a colander over the sink and sprinkle over the salt. Leave for 1 hour to allow water to drain from the courgette.

2. Meanwhile, make the dip by combining all the ingredients in a medium bowl. Set aside.

3. Put the flour in a separate medium bowl. Make a well in the centre and add the beaten egg, stir then add the ricotta, garlic, chilli powder, basil, parsley and some salt. Stir well to combine. Rinse the salt off the courgette and squeeze out any excess water with your hands. Fold the courgette into the mixture.

4. Heat the oil in a 30cm heavy-based frying pan over a medium heat until very hot. To test the temperature, add a tiny piece of courgette; it will sizzle when the oil is hot enough for frying.

5. Spoon the mixture into the hot oil, 1 tablespoon at a time and so the pieces are not touching (it should make 10 fritters). Fry without moving for 4 minutes, then turn and fry for a further 3 minutes or until golden and crispy all over. Remove with a slotted spoon and drain on kitchen paper. Serve 2 warm fritters per person with a dollop of dip on the side.

PANCAKES WITH JERUSALEM ARTICHOKE, LEEK AND CHEESE FILLING

Crespelle Ripiene di Carciofi di Gerusalemme, Porri e Formaggio

Jerusalem artichokes, which are not to be confused with globe artichokes, are the knobbly tubers of plants in the sunflower family. They have nothing to do with Jerusalem; instead, their name derives from the Italian word for sunflower, girasole. *The white flesh is nutty, sweet and a good source of iron. Serve with a crispy salad on the side.*

SERVES 4

115g plain flour
1 large egg
300ml full-fat milk
Pinch of salt
40g salted butter

For the filling
50g salted butter, plus
    extra for greasing
300g Jerusalem artichokes,
    peeled and diced
1 leek, thinly sliced
50g self-raising flour
150g mascarpone cheese
50g freshly grated
    Parmesan cheese
Small handful (about 25g) of
    chopped fresh flat-leaf parsley
Pinch of freshly grated nutmeg
2 large eggs, separated
Salt and freshly ground
    black pepper

1. To make the pancake batter, put the plain flour in a large bowl. Make a well in the centre and add the egg. Pour in the milk gradually, a little at a time, whisking until the flour is completely blended and the mixture is smooth. Add the salt and whisk once more to combine. Cover the batter and leave to rest for half an hour in the fridge.

2. Melt the butter in a 24cm non-stick frying pan over a high heat. Ladle in just enough batter to coat the base and tilt the pan to distribute evenly. Cook for about 1 minute or until the underside of the pancake is golden. Flip over and cook the other side for 30 seconds or until golden then slide it onto a plate. Make 8 thin pancakes in total, reheating the pan before making the next and laying a sheet of baking parchment between each to separate. Set aside.

3. Preheat the oven to 180°C/gas mark 4. Grease a large baking dish with butter.

4. For the filling, melt the butter in a medium saucepan over a medium heat. Add the artichokes and leek and fry gently for 20 minutes or until softened. Season with some salt and pepper. Stir in the self-raising flour and cook for 1 minute. Remove from the heat and mix in the mascarpone, Parmesan, parsley and nutmeg, then stir in the egg yolks.

5. Put the egg whites in a medium bowl and whisk until light and fluffy. Gently fold them into the vegetable mixture using a metal spoon, taking care not to knock out all the air bubbles.

6. Fold each pancake in half, then in half again and lay in the greased baking dish. Spoon the vegetable mixture into the 'pockets' made from the folds. Bake for 18 minutes or until the pancakes are crisp and puffed up. Serve hot.

POTATO RÖSTI AND POACHED EGG WITH FRESH HERB SAUCE

Rösti di Patate con Uova in Camicia e Salsa alle Erbe

A great brunch dish, this takes time to make but the results are well worth the effort. Believe it or not, I've recently started to poach eggs in the microwave. I fill a 300ml heatproof bowl with cold water, gently crack two eggs into it, cover the bowl with cling film and pierce a hole in the top. I then cook them in an 800W microwave on the highest setting for 1 minute and 20 seconds. They cook beautifully! You may find this recipe makes quite a lot of sauce, but I find it's not worth halving the quantities; it's great reheated and served with fish the following day.

SERVES 6

3 large Maris Piper potatoes, about 800g in total, peeled and quartered
100ml vegetable oil
6 medium eggs

For the sauce
200ml double cream
1–2 shallots, peeled and roughly chopped
8 tablespoons fresh flat-leaf parsley
4 tablespoons chopped fresh tarragon
4 tablespoons chopped fresh dill
Salt and white pepper

1. First make the sauce. Blitz all the ingredients in a food processor until smooth and season. Pour into a heatproof bowl and set over a pan of gently simmering water, stirring occasionally, for 15 minutes or until slightly thickened.

2. Put the potatoes in a medium saucepan and cover with cold salted water. Bring to the boil over a high heat then reduce the heat and simmer, covered, for 5 minutes. Drain and leave to cool. When completely cold, grate coarsely into a bowl and season.

3. Dip your hands into cold water to prevent sticking and mould the potato mixture into 6 flat discs, each about the size of your palm. Preheat the oven to its lowest setting. Line 2 baking sheets with baking parchment and set aside.

4. Heat the oil in a 24cm heavy-based, non-stick frying pan over a medium heat. To test the temperature, drop one tiny piece of grated potato into the pan; it will sizzle when the oil is hot enough for frying. Using a fish slice, place 3 of the rösti in the oil and fry for 12 minutes, turning halfway through. Transfer to the lined baking sheets and put in the oven to keep warm while you fry the rest.

5. Poach the eggs, 2 at a time, in a pan of gently simmering salted water for about 3 minutes or in a microwave (see above left). Remove the eggs with a slotted spoon and place on kitchen paper while you poach the remaining eggs. Cover with a lid to keep warm.

6. To serve, spread a small amount of the herb sauce on a plate, lay 2 rösti on it and then carefully place a poached egg on top. Serve immediately.

FENNEL AND LEEK TART WITH PECORINO CHEESE

Torta di Finocchi, Porri e Pecorino

Often called Florence fennel to distinguish it from the herb, fennel is an extremely popular vegetable in Italy. Not only is it frequently used in cooking, but it is sometimes served raw at the end of a meal instead of fruit. It has a strong aniseed flavour, which becomes milder with cooking, and in this recipe its pungency is further tempered by the sweetness of the leeks. If you can't find pecorino sardo, use pecorino romano or Parmesan instead. Serve with a green salad.

SERVES 6

4 tablespoons olive oil
60g salted butter, melted
2 leeks, finely sliced
1 tablespoon fresh thyme leaves
1 fennel bulb, cored and sliced
2 teaspoons fennel seeds
5 large eggs
200ml full-fat milk
150ml double cream
75g freshly grated pecorino
    sardo cheese
300g filo pastry
Salt and freshly ground
    black pepper

1. Preheat the oven to 180°C/gas mark 4. Heat 2 tablespoons of the oil and half the melted butter in a medium frying pan over a medium heat. Add the leeks and thyme and fry gently for 5 minutes, stirring occasionally, until the leeks are tender. Season with some salt and pepper. Tip into a medium bowl and leave to cool.

2. In the same frying pan pour in the remaining oil and fry the fennel slices for 2 minutes each side. Transfer to a plate and leave to cool.

3. Put a heavy-based, dry frying pan over a medium heat. When hot, tip in the fennel seeds and toast for a few minutes. Move the seeds around so they brown evenly and watch that they do not burn. Lightly crush using a pestle and mortar and leave to cool slightly.

4. Beat together the eggs, milk, cream, pecorino and toasted fennel seeds in a medium bowl. Season with black pepper and only a little salt as the cheese is salty.

5. Grease a 25cm loose-bottomed flan tin (ideally fluted) with a little of the remaining melted butter. Line the bottom and sides of the tin with the filo sheets, brushing the rest of the butter between each layer and overlapping the sheets so they cover the tin completely.

6. Spoon the leeks over the bottom of the pastry case and pour over enough egg mixture to cover the leeks. Lay the fennel slices on top and then pour over the remaining egg mixture. Place the tin on a baking sheet and bake for 25–30 minutes or until golden and set.

7. Remove from the oven and leave to cool slightly in its tin. Cut into wedges and serve warm.

PASTA

I can talk about pasta all day long. It's definitely the one thing I'd be happy to eat every day for the rest of my life. There are so many different pasta shapes and, of course, sauces to accompany them. How could anyone ever tire of a perfect plate of pasta?

It's a common belief that you should stay away from pasta if you're trying to lose weight, but Italians are among the healthiest people in the world, with many eating pasta on a daily basis – living proof that it should be part of everybody's weekly diet! Really, it's only certain sauces that are fattening.

You probably know that Italians are sticklers for matching certain types of pasta to certain types of sauce. Basically, the general rule is that smooth, long, thin pasta – like spaghetti, linguine or bucatini – suits a light, oil-based sauce; home-made egg pasta – such as fettuccine or tagliatelle – is best for delicate, creamy sauces; tubular pasta – for instance penne rigate or rigatoni – and pasta shapes that have ridges or twirls – like fusilli and casarecce – go particularly well with a chunkier, thicker sauce, perhaps of rustic vegetables or pulses, to fill their hollows, nooks and crannies. Large pasta shapes – for example, conchiglioni (giant shells) – are good for stuffing and baking.

To cook perfect pasta, bring 5 litres of water to the boil in a large saucepan (ideally 24cm in diameter and at least 18cm tall). Add 2 tablespoons of salt. Immerse the pasta in the boiling water and cook (with the lid off) until al dente. To get the perfect al dente bite, cook the pasta 1 minute less than instructed on the packet. Always toss the cooked pasta in your chosen sauce rather than simply placing the sauce on top, as it allows the flavours to combine better.

Picking my favourite 10 recipes for this chapter was a real struggle – so much so that you have ended up with 16 to choose from! I hope you will enjoy them as much as I do.

Bucatini with Carbonara-style Sauce
and Fried Butternut Squash

Fresh Home-made Orecchiette

Orecchiette with Spicy Roasted Vegetables

Fresh Home-made Egg Pappardelle

Pappardelle with Simple
Mixed Cherry Tomato Sauce

Spaghetti with Pizzaiola Sauce

Neapolitan Pasta Frittata

Spaghetti with Artichokes, Radicchio,
Peas and White Wine

Fusilli with Mascarpone and Yellow
Pepper Sauce with Basil and Rocket

The Ultimate Pasta Bake with Five Cheeses,
Peas and Spinach

Aubergine Lasagne with Capers,
Garlic and Parmesan

Cannelloni Filled with Courgettes,
Ricotta and Provolone Cheese

Venetian-style Pasta Shells Stuffed with
Courgettes and Sage

Baked Penne in Puff Pastry with Leeks,
Mushrooms and Mascarpone

Margherita-style Pasta Salad

Pasta Salad with Spicy Black Olive Pesto

BUCATINI WITH CARBONARA-STYLE SAUCE AND FRIED BUTTERNUT SQUASH

Bucatini con Salsa Stile Carbonara e Zucca Fritta

The tastiest of all the winter squashes, butternut squash is popular for its sweet flavour, vivid colour and creamy texture. It combines surprisingly well with pasta, particularly when fried in butter and olive oil, and is exquisite coated in this rich, carbonara-style sauce. A healthy choice, butternut squash is an excellent source of vitamin A, vitamin C and fibre, as well as carotenoids.

SERVES 4

4 large eggs, lightly beaten
5 tablespoons freshly grated
   pecorino cheese
4 tablespoons chopped fresh
   flat-leaf parsley
4 tablespoons extra virgin
   olive oil
100g salted butter
400g butternut squash, deseeded,
   peeled and cut into 5mm cubes
500g dried bucatini
Salt and freshly ground
   black pepper

1. Combine the beaten eggs, 3 tablespoons of the pecorino, the parsley and plenty of black pepper in a medium bowl. Set aside.

2. Heat the oil and butter in a large frying pan over a medium heat. Add the squash, sprinkle over 3 pinches of salt and fry for 15 minutes, stirring occasionally.

3. Meanwhile, cook the bucatini in a large pan of boiling, salted water until al dente. Drain and tip it back into the same pan, off the heat.

4. Add the squash with the oil and butter, pour over the egg mixture and season with some more salt and pepper. Stir everything together for 30 seconds with a wooden spoon. (The heat from the pasta will be enough to cook the egg through and create a moist, creamy texture.) Serve immediately, sprinkled with the remaining pecorino.

FRESH HOME-MADE ORECCHIETTE

Orecchiette Fatte a Mano

Orecchiette pasta is a speciality of Puglia, in south-eastern Italy, and translates as 'little ears'. It is best served with chunky sauces, such as Spicy Roasted Vegetables (see page 92). Orecchiette are really easy to make and you don't need a pasta machine. Unlike most home-made pastas, which contain eggs, orecchiette dough is made from just flour and tepid water, giving it a firmer texture. Of course, if you're vegan, allergic to eggs or don't like the taste of fresh egg pasta you can use this recipe to make other shapes, too.

**SERVES 4
(MAKES ABOUT 500G)**

400g '00' grade pasta flour, plus
    extra for dusting
2 tablespoons extra virgin olive oil
1/2 teaspoon fine salt

1. Place the flour in a large bowl. Make a well in the centre and pour in the oil and 280ml tepid water and sprinkle over the salt. Using the handle of a wooden spoon, gradually mix the flour into the liquid and stir to combine. Once the texture is crumbly, like breadcrumbs, turn out the mixture onto a well-floured work surface.

2. Knead the mixture until you have a soft, smooth dough (this should take about 8 minutes). The method is the same as for bread: hold the dough in one hand while you fold, push down and stretch the dough away from you with the other hand. Rotate the dough as you go.

3. Divide the dough into pieces and roll them beneath the palms of your hands to make several long 'ropes', each about the thickness of a little finger. Use a sharp knife to cut across to make 1cm pieces. Dust with a little flour.

4. To shape the 'ears', place a piece of dough on a clean wooden board and press into it using your thumb.

5. Place the prepared orecchiette in a single layer on a floured tray until you are ready to cook them. Cook in a large pan of boiling, salted water for about 5 minutes or until they float to the surface.

ORECCHIETTE WITH SPICY ROASTED VEGETABLES

Orecchiette con Verdure Piccanti al Forno

Colourful, nutritious and full of flavour, this is a fantastic dish for any time of year. You can be as creative as you want with your choice of vegetables, but the ones I've chosen really do work amazingly together. They complement each other, rather than fight to be the dominant flavour, and the chilli gives it a great kick.

SERVES 4

1 large red onion, peeled
    and cut into 12 wedges
1 small aubergine, cut into
    1cm cubes
1 large courgette,
    cut into 1cm cubes
2 yellow peppers, deseeded
    and cut into 1cm cubes
2 teaspoons dried chilli flakes
2 tablespoons fresh rosemary
    leaves, finely chopped
10 tablespoons extra virgin
    olive oil
1 head of broccoli, divided
    into bite-sized florets
150ml dry white wine
500g fresh home-made
    orecchiette (see page 90)
40g freshly grated pecorino
    cheese
Salt

1. Preheat the oven to 200°C/gas mark 6. Place the onion in a large, shallow roasting tin with the aubergine, courgette and peppers, sprinkle over the chilli flakes and rosemary and season with some salt. Drizzle over the oil and, using your hands, toss all the vegetables until well coated in the oil.

2. Roast the vegetables for 15 minutes, then add the broccoli. Mix to combine with the other vegetables and to coat the florets in oil. Roast for a further 10 minutes, then pour over the wine. Mix again and return the vegetables to the oven to cook for a further 15 minutes.

3. Meanwhile, cook the orecchiette in a large pan of boiling, salted water for about 5 minutes or until they float to the surface. Drain well and tip them back into the same pan.

4. Add the roasted vegetables and stir all together for about 20 seconds to combine. Finally, sprinkle over the pecorino and serve immediately.

FRESH HOME-MADE EGG PAPPARDELLE

Pappardelle all' Uovo Fatte a Mano

Here I show you how to make fresh egg pasta without a machine. It really isn't difficult and it tastes so delicious. The best flour for making pasta is Italian pasta flour, which is available in most large supermarkets. It gives pasta a more fragrant flavour and delicate texture than other types of flour, it absorbs the eggs more evenly, and it's easier to knead and roll out. If you can't find pasta flour, use strong white flour instead. Pappardelle are the widest of the ribbon pastas. Serve with Simple Mixed Cherry Tomato Sauce (see facing page).

SERVES 4 (MAKES ABOUT 500G)

400g '00' grade pasta flour, plus extra for dusting
4 medium eggs
2 tablespoons extra virgin olive oil
1/2 teaspoon fine salt

1. Place the flour in a large bowl. Make a well in the centre and break in the eggs. Add the oil and salt. Using the handle of a wooden spoon, gradually mix the flour into the liquid and stir to combine. Once the texture is crumbly, like breadcrumbs, turn out the mixture onto a well-floured work surface.

2. Knead the mixture until you have a soft, smooth dough (this should take about 8 minutes). The method is the same as for bread: hold the dough in one hand while you fold, push down and stretch the dough away from you with the other hand. Rotate the dough as you go.

3. Shape the dough into a ball, wrap in cling film and refrigerate for 30 minutes.

4. Dust a rolling pin, the dough and the work surface again with flour to prevent sticking. Flatten the dough with the palm of your hand, then place the rolling pin across one end of the dough and roll it towards the centre. Continue to roll the pin backwards and forwards. Rotate the dough and repeat several times. When the dough has spread out evenly and is so thinly rolled that you can see your hands through it, it's ready.

5. Loosely roll up the sheet of dough to form a flat roll, like a flattened cigar, from one edge to the centre, then repeat from the other edge to the centre. Dust with flour.

6. Using a long, sharp knife, cut across the pasta roll to make 1cm-wide strips. Slide the knife beneath the rolled pasta sheet, lining up the edge of the knife with the centre of the folds. Gently lift the knife so that the pasta ribbons fall down on each side. Toss the pappardelle with a little more flour and cook within the hour in a large pan of boiling, salted water for about 3 minutes or until al dente.

PAPPARDELLE WITH SIMPLE MIXED CHERRY TOMATO SAUCE

Pappardelle con Salsa di Pomodorini Vari

A celebration of tomatoes, this recipe is light, tasty, healthy and yet completely and utterly satisfying. The honey gives it that lovely hint of sweetness and balances the tomatoes' acidity. If you want to give it a little extra kick, add some dried chilli flakes or, even better, make your own chilli oil to pour over the plated dish. It's best to make your own fresh egg pappardelle (see facing page), but if you don't have the time buy a good brand of Italian dried pasta rather than 'fresh pasta' sold in supermarkets, as it will have more flavour.

SERVES 4

5 tablespoons extra
   virgin olive oil
2 garlic cloves, peeled
   and finely sliced
10 fresh yellow cherry
   tomatoes, halved
10 small fresh red plum
   tomatoes, halved
1 tablespoon runny honey
1 x 400g tin of cherry tomatoes
6 fresh basil leaves
500g fresh home-made egg
   pappardelle (see facing page)
Salt and freshly ground
   black pepper

1. Heat the oil in a medium saucepan over a medium heat. Add the garlic, and as soon as it starts to sizzle tip in all the fresh tomatoes. Spoon in the honey, season with some salt and pepper, and fry for 1 minute. Add the tinned tomatoes and basil and cook for 15 minutes, stirring occasionally.

2. Meanwhile, cook the pappardelle in a large pan of boiling, salted water for about 3 minutes or until al dente. Drain well and tip it back into the same pan.

3. Pour over the cherry tomato sauce and stir everything together for about 30 seconds to combine. Check for seasoning and serve immediately.

SPAGHETTI WITH PIZZAIOLA SAUCE

Spaghetti alla Pizzaiola

Spaghetti is best dressed with a light, olive-oil-based sauce that allows the strands to remain slippery and separate. This sauce, based on the ingredients you would use for a pizza topping, makes the ideal partner. I absolutely love the way the cold mozzarella cubes, which are stirred in at the last minute, meet with the hot tomato sauce to transform into a lovely soft melted cheese.

SERVES 4

6 tablespoons extra virgin olive oil
3 garlic cloves, peeled and
    finely sliced
2 tablespoons capers, drained
    and roughly chopped
1 fresh, medium-hot red chilli,
    deseeded and finely sliced
15 pitted Kalamata olives,
    drained and quartered
2 x 400g tins of chopped tomatoes
1 teaspoon dried oregano
500g dried spaghetti
2 x 125g balls of mozzarella cheese,
    drained and cut into 1cm cubes
Salt

1. Heat the oil in a large frying pan over a medium heat. Add the garlic, and as soon as it starts to sizzle add the capers, chilli and olives. Fry for about 30 seconds.

2. Stir in the tomatoes and oregano. Gently simmer for 15 minutes, stirring occasionally. Season with salt, remove from the heat and set aside.

3. Meanwhile, cook the spaghetti in a large pan of boiling, salted water until al dente. Drain well and tip it back into the same pan. Pour over the pizzaiola sauce and stir to combine for about 30 seconds.

4. Divide the pasta between 4 warmed serving plates, scatter over the mozzarella and serve immediately.

NEAPOLITAN PASTA FRITTATA

Frittata Napoletana

Neapolitans love frittata and like to include pasta to make it a really substantial meal. This frittata originated as a way to use up leftovers, but nowadays it is frequently made from freshly cooked ingredients as it is so delicious. It is perfect for a packed lunch or picnic, as well as brunch or a light supper served with salad.

SERVES 4

400g dried penne rigate
5 large eggs
100g fresh baby spinach leaves
10 fresh cherry tomatoes,
    quartered
100g sun-dried tomatoes in oil,
    drained and chopped
2 tablespoons chopped
    fresh chives
60g freshly grated provolone
    piccante cheese
6 tablespoons olive oil
Salt and freshly ground
    black pepper

1. Cook the penne in a large pan of boiling, salted water until al dente. Tip into a colander set over the sink then rinse immediately under cold water. Leave to drain for at least 5 minutes, shaking the colander every minute or so to make sure the pasta doesn't stick.

2. Beat the eggs in a large bowl and add the spinach, cherry tomatoes, sun-dried tomatoes, chives and the provolone piccante. Season with some salt and pepper and mix until thoroughly combined. Stir in the cold penne and leave to rest for 5 minutes, stirring occasionally.

3. Heat the oil in a 26cm heavy-based, non-stick frying pan over a medium heat. Tip in the egg and pasta mixture and tilt the pan a little to spread the ingredients evenly. Fry for 8 minutes without stirring.

4. With the help of a palette knife, gently slide the frittata onto a large, flat plate so that the cooked side is underneath and the uncooked side uppermost. Next, place the frying pan upside down over the plate and quickly but carefully invert both pan and plate so the frittata is inside the pan again. Reduce the heat slightly and fry the uncooked side for a further 8 minutes.

5. Remove the pan from the heat and leave to cool completely. Slice and serve at room temperature. Alternatively, you can serve it cold.

SPAGHETTI WITH ARTICHOKES, RADICCHIO, PEAS AND WHITE WINE

Spaghetti ai Carciofi, Radicchio, Piselli e Vino Bianco

Perfect for a midweek supper, this dish is quick and easy to make and low-fat too. Radicchio is very popular in Italy, particularly in the north, where it grows mainly in the Veneto region. Prized for the rich red colour and slightly bitter flavour of its leaves, radicchio is also a rich source of vitamin K.

SERVES 4

8 tablespoons olive oil
2 red onions, peeled and
   finely sliced
3 tablespoons chopped
   fresh rosemary
12 artichoke hearts in oil,
   drained and quartered
100g frozen peas, defrosted
1 small head of radicchio,
   leaves shredded
100ml dry white wine
500g dried spaghetti
80g Parmesan cheese shavings
Salt and freshly ground
   black pepper

1. Heat the oil in a large frying pan over a medium heat. Add the onions and rosemary and fry gently for 10 minutes, stirring occasionally.

2. Add the artichokes, peas and radicchio, season with salt and pepper and fry for a further 5 minutes, stirring occasionally. Increase the heat, pour in the wine and cook for a further minute so that the alcohol can evaporate.

3. Meanwhile, cook the spaghetti in a large pan of boiling, salted water until al dente. Drain well and tip it back into the same pan. Pour over the vegetables and stir to combine for about 30 seconds.

4. Divide the pasta between 4 warmed serving plates and sprinkle over the Parmesan. Serve immediately.

FUSILLI WITH MASCARPONE AND YELLOW PEPPER SAUCE WITH BASIL AND ROCKET

Fusilli con Salsa di Mascarpone, Peperoni Gialli, Basilico e Rucola

Made from fresh cream, mascarpone is traditionally made in Lombardy, in north-western Italy. It gives this pasta dish a lovely smooth, rich consistency, while the peppers add texture and flavour. You can use red or orange peppers for a slightly sweeter taste if you prefer, but I love the look of the yellow peppers with the red onions. This dish will take you all of 20 minutes to prepare – enjoy!

1. Heat the oil in a medium saucepan over a medium heat. Add the onion and peppers and fry gently for 8 minutes, stirring occasionally.

2. Add the passata and basil, season with salt and pepper and cook for 8 minutes, stirring frequently. Stir in the mascarpone and cook for 2 minutes.

3. Meanwhile, cook the fusilli in a large pan of boiling, salted water until al dente. Drain well and tip it back into the same pan.

4. Pour over the mascarpone sauce, add the rocket and stir everything together for about 30 seconds to combine. Serve immediately.

SERVES 4

6 tablespoons olive oil
1 red onion, peeled and
    finely sliced
2 yellow peppers, deseeded
    and finely sliced
700g passata (sieved tomatoes)
10 fresh basil leaves
250g mascarpone cheese
500g dried wholegrain fusilli
60g rocket leaves
Salt and white pepper

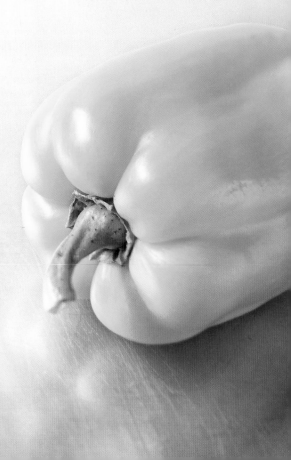

THE ULTIMATE PASTA BAKE WITH FIVE CHEESES, PEAS AND SPINACH

Pasta al Forno ai Cinque Formaggi, Piselli e Spinaci

For all cheese-lovers out there, this is the best-ever comfort food. It has a wickedly creamy, rich texture, yet isn't too heavy, and the peas, spinach and parsley really lift the dish. Please make sure you cook the pasta 2–3 minutes less than stated on the packet, as it will continue to cook in the oven.

SERVES 4–6

350g dried penne rigate
100g freshly grated provolone piccante cheese
100g freshly grated extra-mature Cheddar cheese
100g Gorgonzola piccante cheese, cut into small chunks
100g Taleggio cheese, rind removed and cut into small chunks
3 large egg yolks
150g frozen peas, defrosted
4 tablespoons chopped fresh flat-leaf parsley
100g freshly grated Parmesan cheese
2 large handfuls of baby spinach leaves
Salt and freshly ground black pepper

For the béchamel sauce
50g salted butter
50g plain flour
500ml full-fat milk
Pinch of freshly grated nutmeg

1. Preheat the oven to 200°C/gas mark 6. To make the béchamel sauce, melt the butter in a medium saucepan over a medium heat until foaming. Add the flour and cook for 1–2 minutes until pale golden, stirring continuously. Now start adding the milk a little at a time, whisking constantly and waiting for it to be incorporated before adding more.

2. Bring the sauce to the boil then reduce the heat and simmer gently for 5–10 minutes, whisking occasionally, until thickened and smooth. Add the nutmeg and season with salt and pepper. Remove from the heat and set aside to cool slightly.

3. Cook the penne in a large pan of boiling, salted water for 2–3 minutes less than stated on the packet. Drain well and tip it back into the same pan, off the heat.

4. Pour in the béchamel sauce and add all the cheeses except the Parmesan. Stir everything together for 30 seconds with a wooden spoon. Add the egg yolks, peas, parsley, half the Parmesan and the spinach, and season with a little salt and lots of black pepper. Stir for a further 30 seconds.

5. Tip the pasta into a large baking dish and sprinkle the top with the remaining Parmesan. Bake for 20 minutes until bubbling and blistering on top. Leave to rest out of the oven for 5 minutes before serving.

AUBERGINE LASAGNE WITH CAPERS, GARLIC AND PARMESAN

Lasagne di Melanzane con Capperi, Aglio e Parmigiano

My aubergine lasagne is a great vegetarian dish that also goes down well with meat-eaters. You can prepare it ahead and just pop it in the oven while you're having drinks. If the lasagne sheets are too large to fit in a single layer in your dish, just cut them to fit.

SERVES 6-8

7 tablespoons olive oil
2 large aubergines, cut into
    strips about 3 x 1cm
3 garlic cloves, peeled and
    finely chopped
2 tablespoons capers, drained
    and roughly chopped
3 x 400g tins of chopped tomatoes
1 tablespoon tomato purée
10 fresh basil leaves
12 shop-bought fresh lasagne
    sheets, each about 10 x 18cm
50g freshly grated Parmesan
    cheese
50g salted butter, chilled
    and cut into 1cm cubes
Salt and freshly ground
    black pepper

For the cheese sauce
100g salted butter
100g plain flour
1 litre full-fat milk
50g freshly grated Parmesan
    cheese
1/4 teaspoon freshly grated
    nutmeg

1. Heat the oil in a large frying pan over a medium heat. Add the aubergines, sprinkle over 4 pinches of salt and fry for 15 minutes, stirring occasionally. Add the garlic and capers and fry for 5 minutes. Stir in the tomatoes, tomato purée and basil and simmer for 15 minutes. Season and set aside. Preheat the oven to 180°C/gas mark 4.

2. To make the cheese sauce, melt the butter in a large pan over a medium heat until foaming. Add the flour and cook for 1–2 minutes or until pale golden, stirring continuously. Now add the milk a little at a time, whisking constantly and waiting for it to be incorporated before adding more. Bring to the boil then reduce the heat and simmer for 5–10 minutes, whisking occasionally, until thickened and smooth. Remove from the heat, stir in the Parmesan and add the nutmeg, salt and pepper. Set aside to cool slightly.

3. Spread one-quarter of the cheese sauce over the bottom of a rectangular baking dish measuring about 30 x 25cm. Lay 4 lasagne sheets on the bottom (if necessary, cut them to fit the dish). Spoon over half the aubergine sauce then top with one-third of the remaining cheese sauce.

4. Add another layer of lasagne, cover with the remaining aubergine sauce and spread over half the remaining cheese sauce. Add a final layer of lasagne and spread over all the remaining cheese sauce, covering the lasagne completely. Sprinkle over the Parmesan then scatter over the chilled butter. Grind some black pepper over the top.

5. Place the dish on the bottom shelf of the oven and bake for 30 minutes, then raise it to the middle shelf, increase the temperature to 200°C/gas mark 6 and bake for a further 15 minutes or until golden and crispy. Remove and leave to rest for 10 minutes before serving.

CANNELLONI FILLED WITH COURGETTES, RICOTTA AND PROVOLONE CHEESE

Cannelloni Ripieni di Zucchine, Ricotta e Provolone Piccante

Fresh vegetable cannelloni takes quite a bit of time and concentration to prepare, but I promise you it's worth it. If you want to cheat, you can buy fresh lasagne sheets, which will reduce your preparation time. Here I've used provolone piccante cheese, which has a firm texture and slightly spicy, tangy flavour. If you can't find it, use Parmesan instead.

SERVES 8

720g passata (sieved tomatoes)
4 tablespoons extra virgin
    olive oil
12 fresh basil leaves
50g freshly grated provolone
    piccante cheese
500g fresh egg pasta dough,
    as for Fresh Home-made Egg
    Pappardelle (see page 96)
Salt and white pepper

For the béchamel sauce
100g salted butter
100g plain flour
1 litre full-fat milk
1/4 teaspoon freshly grated nutmeg

For the filling
5 tablespoons olive oil
2 large courgettes,
    cut into 5mm cubes
500g ricotta cheese
100g freshly grated provolone
    piccante cheese
1/4 teaspoon freshly grated nutmeg

1. Pour the passata and extra virgin olive oil into a medium bowl, add the basil and season with some salt and pepper. Stir to combine and set aside.

2. To make the béchamel sauce, melt the butter in a medium saucepan over a medium heat until foaming. Add the flour and cook for 1–2 minutes until pale golden, stirring continuously. Now start adding the milk a little at a time, whisking constantly and waiting for it to be incorporated before adding more. Bring to the boil then reduce the heat and simmer gently for 5–10 minutes, whisking occasionally, until thickened and smooth. Add the nutmeg and season with salt and pepper. Remove from the heat and set aside to cool slightly.

3. To make the filling, heat the olive oil in a large frying pan. Add the courgettes, season with some salt and pepper and fry for 15 minutes over a medium heat, stirring occasionally. Remove from the heat and set aside to cool. Place the cooled courgettes in a large bowl with the remaining ingredients for the filling, season with a little more salt and pepper, and mix using a fork. Cover with cling film and chill in the fridge.

4. Using your fingertips, flatten the pasta dough so that it can fit through the rollers of the pasta machine. Flour the dough on both sides and start to roll it from the widest setting to the thinnest. If you do not have a pasta machine, roll out the pasta dough as thinly as possible using a floured rolling pin until you can see your hands through it. Cut the dough sheet into 26 rectangles measuring about 7 x 15cm.

5. Place a large bowl filled with cold water near the hob and spread out some clean tea towels. Bring a large pan of salted water to the boil. Drop in 5 or 6 rectangles of pasta and cook for 1 minute. Remove with a slotted spoon and transfer to the bowl of water. Leave for 1 minute then remove with a slotted spoon and place in a single layer on the tea towels to dry. Repeat for the remaining pasta.

6. Preheat the oven to 180°C/gas mark 4. Spread 1½ tablespoons of filling over each pasta rectangle, leaving a border of 6mm all round. Starting at one short end, roll up the pasta to enclose the filling, allowing an overlap of about 2cm. Repeat until all the pasta sheets are filled.

7. Spread one-third of the béchamel sauce over the bottom of a rectangular baking dish measuring about 35 x 25cm. Place half the cannelloni on top, with the join underneath, spacing them so they are not touching. Spoon over half the passata mixture and half the remaining béchamel sauce. Add a second layer of cannelloni, spoon over the remaining passata mixture and then the remaining béchamel sauce. Sprinkle over the provolone piccante.

8. Bake for 35 minutes or until golden brown and bubbling. Remove from the oven and leave to rest for 10 minutes before serving.

VENETIAN-STYLE PASTA SHELLS STUFFED WITH COURGETTES AND SAGE

Conchiglioni alla Veneziana

If you're on the lookout for a vegetarian pasta dish that has the 'wow' factor and can be prepared ahead, this is the one for you. When they are stuffed and baked, conchiglioni (giant pasta shells) look so impressive and they taste every bit as good as they look. Fresh sage, which is extremely popular in Italian cooking, gives the dish intriguing, earthy undertones.

SERVES 4

20 conchiglioni (large
    pasta shells)
6 tablespoons olive oil
3 medium courgettes,
    cut into 5mm cubes
1 large onion, peeled
    and finely chopped
6 large fresh sage leaves,
    finely chopped
2 x 400g tins of chopped tomatoes
4 tablespoons chopped fresh
    flat-leaf parsley, plus extra
    to garnish
80g freshly grated pecorino cheese
Salt and freshly ground
    black pepper

For the béchamel sauce
40g salted butter
40g plain flour
400ml full-fat milk
Pinch of freshly grated nutmeg

1. Cook the pasta in a large pan of boiling, salted water for about 5 minutes. Drain and place the shells upside down in a single layer on a clean tea towel to dry.

2. To make the béchamel sauce, melt the butter in a medium saucepan over a medium heat until foaming. Add the flour and cook for 1–2 minutes or until pale golden, stirring continuously. Add the milk a little at a time, whisking constantly and waiting for it to be incorporated before adding more. Bring to the boil then reduce the heat and simmer for 5–10 minutes, whisking occasionally, until thickened and smooth. Add the nutmeg and season. Remove from the heat and set aside to cool slightly.

3. Heat the oil in a large frying pan over a medium heat. Add the courgettes, onion and sage and sprinkle over 2 pinches of salt. Fry gently for 10 minutes, stirring occasionally. Transfer to a heatproof bowl and set aside to cool slightly. Preheat the oven to 190°C/gas mark 5.

4. Tip the tomatoes into a small saucepan and bring to the boil. Reduce the heat and add the parsley and seasoning. Simmer for 8 minutes, stirring occasionally. Reserve 6 tablespoons of the sauce and spread the rest over the bottom of a baking dish measuring about 25 x 25cm.

5. Add half the béchamel sauce to the courgettes. Using a tablespoon, fill the pasta shells with the courgette mixture. Lay the shells in a single layer in the dish, stuffed-side up and not touching. Spoon the remaining béchamel over each shell. Cover with foil and bake for 15–20 minutes. Sprinkle with the pecorino and bake uncovered for a further 5 minutes or until golden. Let rest for 3 minutes. Garnish with parsley and pepper. To serve, spoon some of the reserved sauce on each plate and lay 5 shells on top.

BAKED PENNE IN PUFF PASTRY WITH LEEKS, MUSHROOMS AND MASCARPONE

Penne al Forno in Pasta Frolla con Porri, Funghi e Mascarpone

In southern Italy, pasta is sometimes baked in a pastry crust. Here I've come up with my own version, combining penne with a creamy sauce of mushrooms, leeks and cheese and enclosing it in puff pastry. The flaky texture of the pastry contrasts so beautifully with the soft filling and the flavours are amazing. Another great thing about this dish is that you can make the pasta and sauce ahead, and when you're ready to eat simply fill the pastry case and pop it in the oven. It's a good way to use up leftover pasta too.

SERVES 4

80g salted butter, plus extra
    for greasing
250g chestnut mushrooms, sliced
2 medium leeks, sliced 5mm thick
2 garlic cloves, peeled and
    finely chopped
250g mascarpone cheese
3 tablespoons chopped
    fresh chives
4 pinches of cayenne pepper
100g freshly grated Parmesan
    cheese
300g dried penne rigate
1 x 320g block of shop-
    bought puff pastry
20ml milk
Salt

1. Melt the butter in a large frying pan over a medium heat. Add the mushrooms, leeks and garlic and fry for 8 minutes, stirring occasionally. Add the mascarpone and cook for a further minute, stirring continuously. Mix in the chives, cayenne pepper, half the Parmesan cheese and salt to taste. Transfer to a large heatproof bowl.

2. Preheat the oven to 190°C/gas mark 5. Cook the penne in a large pan of boiling, salted water for 2–3 minutes less than stated on the packet (it will continue to cook in the oven). Drain well and tip it into the bowl with the mascarpone sauce. Stir to combine and leave to cool.

3. Meanwhile, grease a 24cm round springform tin or loose-bottomed cake tin and line with the puff pastry. Prick the pastry all over with a fork and tip the pasta mixture into the pastry case.

4. Brush the inside of the pastry case with milk and gently fold over the sides of the case so that the excess pastry touches the pasta. Brush the exposed surface of the pastry with milk. Sprinkle over the remaining Parmesan. Bake for 20 minutes until crispy and golden. Serve hot.

MARGHERITA-STYLE PASTA SALAD

Insalata di Fusilli Stile Margherita

This is one of my favourite pasta salads: the colours (green, red and white, like the Italian flag) remind me of home and it is so easy to make, yet looks stunning and tastes really delicious. I have served it in many ways – as a starter, an accompaniment, with other salads at a barbecue and as a packed lunch – and it always vanishes within minutes. A must-try!

SERVES 4

400g dried fusilli
10 fresh red cherry
   tomatoes, halved
10 fresh yellow cherry
   tomatoes, halved
3 x 125g balls of mozzarella,
   drained and cut into 1cm cubes
15 fresh basil leaves, shredded
8 tablespoons extra virgin
   olive oil
Salt and freshly ground
   black pepper

1. Cook the fusilli in a large pan of boiling, salted water until al dente. Tip into a colander set over the sink then rinse immediately under cold running water. Leave to drain for at least 5 minutes, shaking the colander every minute or so to make sure the pasta doesn't stick.

2. Place the red and yellow cherry tomatoes, mozzarella and basil in a large bowl. Pour over the oil and season with some salt and pepper. Mix with a tablespoon and set aside for about 15 minutes to allow the flavours to combine, stirring occasionally.

3. Add the fusilli to the bowl with the tomato and mozzarella mixture and gently stir everything together until the pasta is coated in the mixture. Cover with cling film and leave to rest at room temperature for 10 minutes, stirring every few minutes.

PASTA SALAD WITH SPICY BLACK OLIVE PESTO

Insalata di Fusilli al Pesto Piccante di Olive Nere

Purple-black Kalamata olives make an intensely flavoured pesto that can be used on pasta or as a spread or a dip. Here I've combined it with fusilli and chargrilled peppers to make a delicious pasta salad. I love the simplicity of this recipe – just a few ingredients blitzed together and you end up with such strong flavours. This is Italian food at its best: fresh, easy and amazing!

SERVES 4

500g dried fusilli
250g pitted Kalamata
   olives, drained
2 garlic cloves, peeled
30g capers, drained
1 teaspoon dried chilli flakes
3 tablespoons roughly chopped
   fresh flat-leaf parsley
5 tablespoons extra virgin olive oil
2 tablespoons freshly squeezed
   lemon juice
150g chargrilled red and yellow
   peppers in a jar, drained
   and thinly sliced
Large bag of mixed Italian-style
   salad leaves to serve
Chilli oil for drizzling

1. Cook the fusilli in a large pan of boiling, salted water until al dente. Tip into a colander set over the sink then rinse immediately under cold running water. Leave to drain for at least 5 minutes, shaking the colander every minute or so to make sure the pasta doesn't stick.

2. To make the olive pesto, place the olives, garlic, capers, chilli flakes and parsley in a food processor. Pour in the olive oil and the lemon juice and blitz until you create a smooth paste. If the mixture is too dry, add some cold water to make it smoother. Transfer to a large bowl.

3. Add the fusilli and peppers and gently stir everything together until the pasta is coated in the mixture. Cover with cling film and leave to rest at room temperature for 10 minutes, stirring halfway.

4. Arrange the salad leaves on a large serving platter. Stir the pasta once more then spoon it over the leaves. Drizzle all over with a little chilli oil.

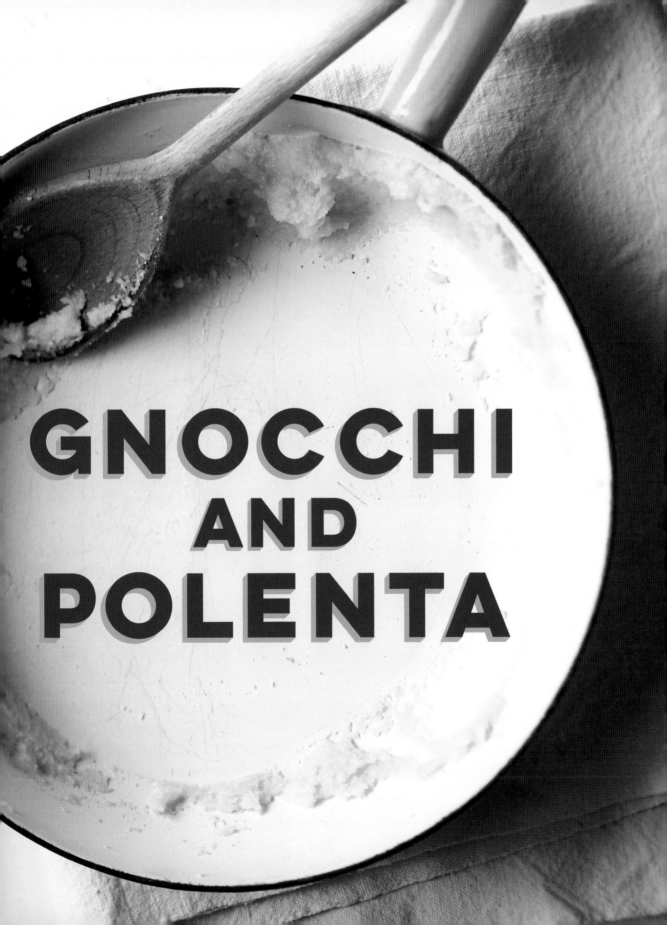

GNOCCHI AND POLENTA

Please don't look at the subject of this chapter – then skip through the pages and quickly move on to the next section! Maybe you've tried gnocchi and polenta in restaurants and found them stodgy or tasteless, but I can assure you that it will have been because they haven't been cooked in the right way. Correctly prepared, they are a culinary delight.

In Italy, we tend to serve gnocchi (little dumplings) as a first course alternative to soup or pasta. Like pasta, gnocchi are boiled or baked and served with any number of sauces. Typically made with potatoes and flour, they can also include cheese or spinach; if you're buying ready-made gnocchi, be sure to select a product that contains at least 70 per cent potato for the best results. Remember – whether you're making them from scratch or using shop-bought gnocchi, never overcook them as they will have a soggy texture.

Another popular carb in Italy, particularly in the north, is polenta (yellow maize flour). It is a fantastic ingredient that can be used in savoury or sweet dishes and makes a refreshing alternative to potatoes, pasta and rice. It can be simply boiled and served with a sauce, or boiled then baked or fried to give a completely different consistency. It is also a good choice for those requiring a gluten-free diet – many coeliacs use uncooked polenta instead of breadcrumbs or as an alternative to flour when baking cakes and biscuits.

I have chosen a few of my favourite gnocchi and polenta recipes for this book, as both make a great base for vegetables, and urge you to try just one of each. Once you have, I know you'll want to try the rest!

Gnocchi with Roasted Tomato Sauce

Gnocchi with a Creamy Mushroom
and Pea Sauce

Sweet Potato Gnocchi with Sage
and Amaretti Biscuits

Baked Gnocchi with Cannellini Beans,
Spinach and Tomatoes

Cheesy Polenta with Spicy Roasted
Aubergine Sauce

Saffron Polenta with Sweet Pepper,
Olive and Caper Sauce

Fried Polenta with Baked Cheesy
Mushrooms and Parsley Butter

Baked Spinach Polenta with Vegetable Ragu

GNOCCHI WITH ROASTED TOMATO SAUCE

Gnocchi Fatti in Casa con Salsa di Pomodori al Forno

I love the simplicity and wholesomeness of fresh, home-made gnocchi and roasted tomato sauce. When tomatoes are in season they taste so much better and their price drops, so it's a great time to buy large quantities or use up the ones that are starting to over-ripen. I often make a big batch of this sauce in summer, use some for this dish and freeze the rest for another day.

SERVES 6

2kg fresh ripe tomatoes, halved
3 garlic cloves, peeled and sliced
5 sprigs of fresh thyme
4 tablespoons extra virgin
    olive oil
1kg floury potatoes, such as
    Desirée or Maris Piper,
    scrubbed
100g '00' grade pasta flour or plain
    flour, plus extra for dusting
2 medium egg yolks
60g Parmesan cheese shavings
12 fresh basil leaves
Salt and freshly ground
    black pepper

1. Preheat the oven to 180°C/gas mark 4. Scatter the tomatoes, garlic and thyme in a large, shallow roasting tin. Drizzle over the oil, season and toss together. Prick the skins of the potatoes in several places. Place the roasting tin and the potatoes directly on the middle shelf of the oven and cook for 1 hour.

2. Remove the tin and potatoes from the oven and leave to cool slightly. Discard the thyme and tip the tomatoes, garlic and juices into a blender or food processor and blitz until smooth. Transfer the mixture to a medium saucepan, check for seasoning and simmer very gently over a low heat for 10 minutes, stirring occasionally. Set aside.

3. Meanwhile, cut the cooled potatoes in half. Scrape out the flesh and pass it through a potato ricer set over a large bowl or mash until very smooth. Add the flour and seasoning, then make a well and add the egg yolks. Mix to a smooth dough using the handle of a wooden spoon.

4. Divide the dough into two equal-sized pieces. On a lightly floured surface, roll each piece beneath the palms of your hands into a long sausage shape about 1.5cm thick. Use a sharp knife to cut across into 2cm lengths.

5. Bring a large pan of salted water to the boil. Meanwhile, gently reheat the tomato sauce over a low heat.

6. Drop the gnocchi into the boiling water and cook for about 2 minutes or until they float to the surface. Drain thoroughly and tip them back into the same pan. Pour over three-quarters of the tomato sauce (the remaining can be frozen for another dish) and stir gently for 30 seconds to combine. To serve, spoon onto warm plates, scatter over the Parmesan and basil and serve immediately.

GNOCCHI WITH A CREAMY MUSHROOM AND PEA SAUCE

Gnocchi con Crema di Funghi e Piselli

Mushrooms and peas are a classic combination, particularly delicious in a creamy wine sauce. I learnt this recipe at catering college in Naples and well remember my teacher telling me all about the virtues of frozen peas. I can still hear him warning me against cooking them for too long; they lose their bright green colour and crisp texture. For variety, replace the Parmesan with a blue cheese.

SERVES 4

1kg floury potatoes, such as
   Desirée or Maris Piper, peeled
   and cut into 5cm chunks
100g '00' grade pasta flour or plain
   flour, plus extra for dusting
2 medium egg yolks

For the sauce
4 tablespoons olive oil
1 echalion (banana) shallot,
   peeled and finely chopped
400g mixed wild mushrooms,
   large ones cut in half
100ml white wine
300ml double cream
4 tablespoons freshly grated
   Parmesan cheese
200g frozen peas, defrosted
2 tablespoons chopped
   fresh chives
Salt and freshly ground
   black pepper

1. Put the potatoes in a large pan and cover with cold, salted water. Bring to the boil then simmer for 15–20 minutes or until tender. Drain well and leave for 2–3 minutes then pass through a potato ricer set over a large bowl or mash using a potato masher until really smooth. Set aside.

2. To make the sauce, heat the oil in a medium frying pan over a high heat. Add the shallot and fry for 1 minute, stirring, then add the mushrooms and fry for 3 minutes. Pour in the wine and simmer until reduced by half. Pour in the cream and simmer for 2 minutes. Season with salt and pepper, stir to combine and remove the pan from the heat. Set aside.

3. Add the flour to the mashed potatoes, season, then make a well and add the egg yolks. Mix thoroughly to form a soft, smooth dough using the handle of a wooden spoon.

4. Divide the dough in half. On a lightly floured surface, roll each piece with your hands into a long sausage shape about 1.5cm thick. Use a sharp knife to cut across into 2cm lengths. Roll the back of a fork over one side of each piece to get the grooved imprint from the prongs. Lay the gnocchi on a floured tray until ready to cook.

5. Bring a large pan of salted water to the boil. Meanwhile, place the sauce over a gentle heat and add the Parmesan, peas and chives. Check for seasoning and stir.

6. Drop the gnocchi into the boiling water and cook for about 2 minutes or until they float to the surface. Reserve a ladleful of the cooking water. Drain the gnocchi then tip into the mushroom sauce with about 2 tablespoons of the reserved cooking water to loosen the sauce. Stir gently for 30 seconds to combine. Serve immediately.

SWEET POTATO GNOCCHI WITH SAGE AND AMARETTI BISCUITS

Gnocchi di Patata Dolce con Salvia e Amaretti

Brown butter and sage make quite a common pairing in Italy, particularly in the northern region of Emilia Romagna. I like to serve it with gnocchi made from a mixture of potatoes and sweet potatoes, and sprinkle over crushed amaretti biscuits to give a little extra crunch and flavour. If you prefer, you can use butternut squash instead of sweet potatoes for this recipe.

SERVES 4

500g floury potatoes, such
    as Desirée or Maris Piper,
    scrubbed
500g sweet potatoes, scrubbed
200g '00' grade pasta flour
    or plain flour, plus extra
    for dusting
2 medium egg yolks
70g salted butter
20 small fresh sage leaves
Grated zest of 1 lemon and
    1 teaspoon juice
8 amaretti biscuits, crushed
Salt and white pepper

1. Preheat the oven to 180°C/gas mark 4. Prick the skins of the potatoes and sweet potatoes in several places. Bake the sweet potatoes for about 50 minutes and the potatoes for about 1¼ hours or until cooked through (the length of time they take to cook depends on their size). Remove from the oven and set aside to cool slightly.

2. As soon as the potatoes and sweet potatoes are cool enough to handle, cut them in half. Scrape out the flesh and pass it through a potato ricer set over a large bowl or mash using a potato masher until really smooth. Add the flour and season with salt and pepper, then make a well and add the egg yolks. Mix thoroughly to form a soft, smooth dough using the handle of a wooden spoon.

3. Divide the dough into two equal-sized pieces. On a lightly floured surface, roll each piece beneath the palms of your hands into a long sausage shape about 3cm wide. Use a sharp knife to cut across into 2cm lengths.

4. Bring a large pan of salted water to the boil. Meanwhile, heat the butter in a large frying pan over a medium heat until lightly golden. Add the sage and the lemon zest and juice, stir then remove from the heat and set aside.

5. Drop the gnocchi into the boiling water and cook for about 30 seconds or until they float to the surface. Reserve a ladleful of the cooking water. Drain the gnocchi well then tip into the frying pan and stir to coat in the butter. Add a little of the reserved cooking water (about 2 tablespoons) to create a sauce and season. Return the pan to a medium heat and stir gently for 30 seconds. To serve, spoon onto warm plates and sprinkle over the amaretti biscuits.

BAKED GNOCCHI WITH CANNELLINI BEANS, SPINACH AND TOMATOES

Gnocchi al Forno con Cannellini, Spinaci e Pomodori

I love making fresh gnocchi with my kids, but sometimes I simply don't have the time so I buy them instead. When buying gnocchi, look for a good-quality brand that contains at least 70 per cent potato. Baking shop-bought gnocchi can really jazz them up. Here I've combined them with spinach, cherry tomatoes, cannellini beans and cheese for a hearty dish. Serve with a crisp salad on the side.

SERVES 4

4 tablespoons olive oil,
   plus extra for greasing
2 garlic cloves, peeled and sliced
500g fresh cherry tomatoes
   (red and yellow), halved
50ml dry white wine
1 x 400g tin of cannellini beans,
   rinsed and drained
450g baby spinach leaves
500g shop-bought gnocchi
   (minimum 70% potato)
1 x 125g ball of mozzarella
   cheese, drained and cut
   into small pieces
50g freshly grated Parmesan
   cheese
Salt and freshly ground
   black pepper

1. Preheat the oven to 200°C/gas mark 6. Grease a baking dish, measuring about 20 x 20cm, and set aside. Bring a large pan of salted water to the boil.

2. Meanwhile, heat the oil in a large frying pan over a medium heat. Add the garlic, and as soon as it starts to sizzle add the tomatoes and fry for 1 minute. Pour in the wine and simmer gently until the tomatoes 'pop' and release their juices. Tip in the beans and reduce the heat. Allow everything to warm through then add the spinach and cook briefly until wilted. Season with salt and pepper.

3. Drop the gnocchi into the boiling water and cook for 2–3 minutes or until they float to the surface. Reserve a ladleful of the cooking water. Drain the gnocchi and tip into the sauce. Pour in about 2 tablespoons of the reserved cooking water to loosen the sauce and stir to combine.

4. Spoon the gnocchi into the greased baking dish then scatter over the mozzarella and Parmesan. Bake for about 10 minutes or until golden. Serve hot.

CHEESY POLENTA WITH SPICY ROASTED AUBERGINE SAUCE

Polenta al Formaggio con Melanzane Piccanti al Forno

Aubergines are so versatile; they can be cooked in many ways and are used in a vast range of dishes, both hot and cold. For this dish, I have roasted the aubergines so that they maintain some of their texture and intensify in flavour, combining beautifully with the Parmesan in the polenta. Make sure to buy 'quick-cook' polenta; the traditional type requires a lot more cooking and stirring.

SERVES 4

600ml vegetable stock
150ml full-fat milk
150g quick-cook polenta
50g salted butter
100g freshly grated
    Parmesan cheese
2 tablespoons chopped
    fresh flat-leaf parsley

For the sauce
4 medium aubergines,
    cut into 2cm cubes
8 tablespoons olive oil
1 red onion, peeled and
    finely sliced
2 teaspoons dried chilli flakes
2 x 400g tins of chopped tomatoes
Salt

1. First make the sauce. Preheat the oven to 190°C/gas mark 5. Scatter the aubergines in a large, shallow roasting tin, drizzle over half the oil, season with salt and toss to coat the aubergines thoroughly in the oil. Roast for 30 minutes, turning the aubergines halfway through cooking.

2. Meanwhile, heat the remaining oil in a medium saucepan over a medium heat. Add the onion and chilli flakes and fry gently for 8 minutes. Tip in the tomatoes and cook gently for 10 minutes, stirring occasionally. Stir in the aubergines and season with salt. Keep warm.

3. Pour the stock and milk into a large saucepan and bring to the boil over a high heat. Reduce the heat to a simmer and gradually add the polenta, whisking continually and vigorously until it starts to thicken and bubble. Simmer for 4 minutes, stirring occasionally. Remove from the heat, season with salt and stir in the butter and Parmesan.

4. To serve, spoon the polenta into warm bowls or onto plates, top with the aubergine sauce and scatter over the chopped parsley.

SAFFRON POLENTA WITH SWEET PEPPER, OLIVE AND CAPER SAUCE

Polenta allo Zafferano con Salsa di Peperoni Dolci, Olive e Capperi

The world's most expensive spice, saffron imbues polenta with a soft golden colour and characteristic delicate flavour. Here I've topped saffron polenta with a piquant, sweet red pepper sauce to make a vibrant combination. If you like your sauces creamy, add mascarpone to the peppers.

SERVES 4

400ml vegetable stock
350ml full-fat milk
1 pinch of saffron threads
150g quick-cook polenta
80g salted butter
2 tablespoons chopped
    fresh flat-leaf parsley

For the sauce
6 tablespoons olive oil
2 red onions, peeled and sliced
2 red peppers, deseeded
    and thinly sliced
2 yellow peppers, deseeded
    and thinly sliced
80g pitted Kalamata olives,
    drained and halved
1 tablespoon capers, drained
3 tablespoons red wine vinegar
Salt and freshly ground
    black pepper

1. First make the sauce. Heat the oil in a large sauté pan or frying pan with a lid over a medium heat. Add the onions and peppers and fry gently for 10 minutes, then tip in the olives and capers and cook for 15 minutes, stirring occasionally. Pour in the vinegar and stir in some salt and pepper. Cover and cook for 5 minutes. Remove from the heat and keep warm.

2. Put the stock, milk and saffron in a large saucepan and bring to the boil over a high heat. Reduce the heat to a simmer and gradually add the polenta, whisking continually and vigorously until it starts to thicken and bubble. Simmer for 4 minutes, stirring occasionally. Remove from the heat, season with salt and pepper and stir in the butter.

3. To serve, spoon the polenta into warm bowls or onto plates, top with the pepper sauce and scatter over the chopped parsley.

FRIED POLENTA WITH BAKED CHEESY MUSHROOMS AND PARSLEY BUTTER

Polenta Fritta con Funghi al Formaggio e Burro Aromatico

This is a great lunch recipe and a perfect way of using up leftover polenta. It can be bland on its own, but is a real treat if topped with meaty-textured, inky Portobello mushrooms that have been topped with cheese and baked. Serve with a side salad.

SERVES 4

600ml vegetable stock
150ml full-fat milk
150g quick-cook polenta
50g freshly grated pecorino
   cheese
8 Portobello mushrooms
10 tablespoons olive oil,
   plus extra for greasing
1 tablespoon chopped fresh
   rosemary
150g Taleggio cheese,
   rind removed and cut
   into small pieces
50g salted butter
2 spring onions, thinly sliced
2 tablespoons chopped fresh
   flat-leaf parsley
Salt and freshly ground
   black pepper

1. Preheat the oven to 180°C/gas mark 4. Line a shallow roasting tin, measuring about 20 x 30cm, with a double layer of cling film. Set aside.

2. Pour the stock and milk into a large saucepan and bring to the boil over a high heat. Reduce the heat to a simmer and gradually add the polenta, whisking continually and vigorously until it starts to thicken and bubble. Simmer for 4 minutes, stirring occasionally. Remove from the heat, season with salt and pepper and stir in the pecorino. Spoon the cooked polenta into the lined roasting tin and set aside to cool and set.

3. Place the mushrooms on an oiled baking sheet. Drizzle over 4 tablespoons of the oil, scatter over the rosemary and season with some salt and pepper. Bake for 10 minutes, then top with the Taleggio and cook for a further 5 minutes.

4. Meanwhile, heat the butter in a small saucepan over a medium heat. Add the spring onions and parsley and fry for 2 minutes. Set aside and keep warm. Cut the set polenta into quarters.

5. Heat the remaining oil in a large frying pan over a medium heat. Add the polenta and fry for 2 minutes each side until golden and crispy.

6. To serve, lay each piece of polenta in the centre of a plate and top with 2 baked mushrooms. Drizzle over some of the flavoured butter. Serve immediately.

BAKED SPINACH POLENTA WITH VEGETABLE RAGU

Polenta al Forno con Spinaci e Ragù di Verdure

Spinach is often used in Italian cooking to add colour and flavour to otherwise bland carbohydrates such as pasta, gnocchi and, in this case, polenta. As well as spinach, this nutritious bake is packed full of other vegetables too, and topped with an irresistible creamy, cheesy topping. I came up with this idea as I wanted to create an unusual alternative to vegetarian lasagne, and I think it fits the bill perfectly.

SERVES 4

225g frozen spinach,
   defrosted and drained
600ml vegetable stock
150ml full-fat milk
165g quick-cook polenta
5 tablespoons olive oil
1 onion, peeled and finely chopped
1 aubergine, cut into 1cm chunks
4 courgettes (2 green, 2 yellow),
   cut into 1cm chunks
1 teaspoon dried oregano
1 x 400g tin of chopped tomatoes
300ml crème fraîche
100g freshly grated Parmesan
   cheese
100g ready-grated mozzarella
   cheese
Salt and freshly ground
   black pepper

1. Preheat the oven to 190°C/gas mark 5. Squeeze as much liquid as you can out of the spinach and roughly chop.

2. Pour the stock and milk into a large saucepan and bring to the boil over a high heat. Reduce the heat to a simmer and gradually add the polenta, whisking continually and vigorously until it starts to thicken and bubble. Simmer for 4 minutes, stirring occasionally.

3. Add the spinach and heat through for 3–5 minutes. Season with some salt and pepper. Spoon the mixture into a baking dish measuring about 20 x 20cm. Set aside.

4. Heat the oil in a large frying pan over a medium heat. Add the onion and fry gently for 5 minutes, then add the aubergine and fry for 2 minutes, then the courgettes and fry for 15 minutes. Stir occasionally. Sprinkle over the oregano and pour in the chopped tomatoes. Stir and simmer gently for 10 minutes. Spoon the vegetables over the polenta.

5. In a small bowl, combine the crème fraîche, Parmesan and a few grindings of pepper. Spoon the mixture over the vegetables and sprinkle over the mozzarella. Bake for 20–25 minutes or until bubbling and golden. Serve hot.

PIZZA
AND
PIES

I come from southern Italy, where a week never goes by when we don't enjoy a slice of pizza ... or three ... The best pizzas are generally made in a traditional clay oven, but you can create something fantastic in a conventional kitchen oven too. As I always say: when cooking, the secret of success lies in using the very best ingredients you can find.

Home-made pizzas are a winner with everyone – particularly children. Guests are always impressed that I've made them from scratch, yet they're among my easiest recipes. The same applies to my calzone recipes (a calzone is basically a topped pizza folded in half and sealed – *calzone* literally means 'stocking' or 'trouser'). These make an exciting change to pizza, and there is always the added surprise element of what is contained inside the crust.

I also wanted to include some of my favourite savoury pies and tarts in this chapter. Known as *torte*, pies are found all over Italy – but they are a particular speciality of the Liguria province on the Italian Riviera. This is because, traditionally, Liguria is not a wheat-producing area so flour in that region used to be scarce and expensive; consequently, the locals would make pies rather than pasta as pastry requires less flour. They filled the pies with local produce, such as seasonal vegetables, eggs and cheese. Strictly speaking, tarts have a single crust (like a quiche), while pies are double-crusted – but otherwise, they're pretty much the same thing. And delicious though they are when served hot, they are also great when eaten cold the next day.

Pizza Topped with Four Cheeses,
Courgette and Fresh Basil

Pizza Tray with a Chargrilled Pepper,
Olive and Caper Topping

The Best Gluten-free Pizza Ever

Pizza Cake with Semi-dried Tomatoes,
Spinach and Goat's Cheese

Fried Pizza with Mozzarella and Fresh Basil

Super-spicy Calzone with Sweet Peppers
and Olives

Calzone with Ricotta, Pecorino,
Mozzarella, Tomato and Pesto

Cavolo Nero, Rocket and Artichoke Tart
with Provolone Cheese

Roasted Vegetable Pie with Lemon Zest
and Fresh Rosemary

Spinach, Rocket and Cheese Pie
with a Hint of Chilli

PIZZA TOPPED WITH FOUR CHEESES, COURGETTE AND FRESH BASIL

Pizza ai Quattro Formaggi, Zucchine e Basilico

Classic and highly indulgent, the Quattro Formaggi *pizza is sublime. However, I decided to give it a new twist by adding courgettes, which help to cut the richness of the cheeses as well as adding colour, flavour and texture. You can, of course, use other cheeses if you prefer.*

MAKES 2

200g strong white flour,
    plus extra for dusting
1 x 7g sachet fast-action
    (easy blend) dried yeast
3/4 teaspoon salt
2 tablespoons extra virgin olive
    oil, plus extra for greasing

For the topping
150g mascarpone cheese
150g ricotta cheese
1 small, young courgette
100g freshly grated pecorino
    cheese
150g Gorgonzola cheese
    (chilled), cut into small cubes
1 tablespoon extra virgin olive oil
10 fresh basil leaves
Salt and freshly ground
    black pepper

1. Place the flour in a large bowl. Add the yeast to one side of the bowl and the salt to the other. Make a well in the centre and add the oil then gradually pour in 140ml warm water and mix together using the handle of a wooden spoon.

2. Knead the dough on a lightly floured surface for about 5 minutes or until soft, smooth and elastic.

3. Shape the dough into a round and place in a large oiled bowl. Brush the top with a little oil and cover with cling film. Leave to rest at room temperature for 20 minutes. Brush 2 baking sheets with oil and set aside. Preheat the oven to 220°C/gas mark 7.

4. Turn out the dough onto a lightly floured surface and knead just 3 or 4 times to knock out the air. Halve the dough and roll out each half directly onto an oiled baking sheet, rolling and stretching the dough to make 2 rounds about 25cm in diameter and 1–2cm thick. Make a small rim by pulling up the edges slightly.

5. To make the topping, combine the mascarpone and ricotta in a medium bowl and season with salt and pepper. Spread the mixture over the top of the pizza bases, avoiding the rim.

6. Use a vegetable peeler or mandolin to shave the courgette lengthways into long, thin strips and arrange on the surface of the pizzas. Scatter over the pecorino and Gorgonzola. Drizzle with the oil.

7. Bake for 14 minutes or until golden brown. Remove from the oven, scatter over the basil and return to the oven for 1 further minute. Serve hot.

PIZZA TRAY WITH A CHARGRILLED PEPPER, OLIVE AND CAPER TOPPING

Pizzona con Peperoni Grigliati, Olive e Capperi

Ideal for sharing, this is a large, almost focaccia-style pizza and is perfect for a night in with friends or family. I have served this as an anti-pasto too, and it works well. If you have a very hungry group, it would be a good idea to make two batches of this pizza, as the slices go quickly!

SERVES 8

500g strong white flour,
   plus extra for dusting
1 x 7g sachet fast-action
   (easy blend) dried yeast
2 teaspoons salt
3 tablespoons extra virgin olive
   oil, plus extra for greasing

For the topping
300g passata (sieved tomatoes)
290g mixed chargrilled peppers
   in a jar, drained and sliced
20 pitted Kalamata olives, drained
1 tablespoon capers, drained
2 teaspoons dried oregano
1/2 teaspoon dried chilli flakes
3 tablespoons extra virgin
   olive oil

1. Place the flour in a large bowl. Add the yeast to one side of the bowl and the salt to the other. Make a well in the centre and add the oil then gradually pour in 300ml warm water and mix together using the handle of a wooden spoon.

2. Knead the dough on a lightly floured surface for about 10 minutes or until soft, smooth and elastic, adding a little more flour if it's really sticky.

3. Shape the dough into a round and place in a large oiled bowl. Brush the top with a little oil. Cover with cling film and leave to rise in a warm, draught-free place for about 1 hour or until doubled in size. Brush a large baking sheet with oil and set aside.

4. Turn out the dough onto a lightly floured surface, knead just 3 or 4 times to knock out the air and transfer to an oiled traybake tin measuring about 30 x 23cm. Using your fingertips, gently flatten the dough to extend to the sides (it should be about 1cm thick) and press your fingertips into the dough to create indentations. Brush over a little oil, cover with a tea towel and leave to rise again in a warm place for a further 20 minutes. Preheat the oven to 220°C/gas mark 6.

5. Remove the cling film and make more indentations in the dough. Spread over the passata, leaving a 1cm border all round. Scatter over the peppers, olives and capers, and sprinkle over the oregano and chilli flakes. Drizzle the top with the oil.

6. Bake for 18 minutes or until golden brown. Transfer to a wire rack to cool slightly. Cut into 8 slices and serve hot.

THE BEST GLUTEN-FREE PIZZA EVER

La Migliore Pizza in Assoluto Senza Glutine

I have often been told that gluten-free pizzas aren't as good as pizzas made with ordinary flour, and I hope to change that with this recipe. The inspiration for the topping came from my son, who would eat avocado and tomato salad with balsamic vinegar every day if he could! I love the fact there are so many fresh, raw vegetables on it, and the combination of hot and cold – the balance is perfect.

MAKES 2

2 tablespoons extra virgin olive
   oil, plus extra for greasing
200g gluten-free flour
1 x 7g sachet fast-action
   (easy blend) dried yeast
1/2 teaspoon salt
1 tablespoon fresh thyme leaves
Freshly ground black pepper

For the topping
400ml passata (sieved tomatoes)
1 x 125g ball of mozzarella
   cheese, drained and cut
   into small pieces
1/2 ripe avocado, halved, stoned,
   peeled and thickly sliced
10 fresh yellow cherry
   tomatoes, halved
60g rocket leaves
Balsamic glaze for drizzling

1. Preheat the oven to 220°C/gas mark 7. Brush 2 baking sheets with oil. Set aside.

2. Place the flour, yeast, salt, thyme and a little black pepper into a food processor and add the oil. Pulse until all the ingredients are combined. With the blades still turning, pour in enough warm water (about 140ml) to make a soft dough.

3. Tip the dough onto a floured surface and knead for 5 minutes or until smooth and elastic. Halve the dough and roll out each half directly onto the oiled baking sheets, rolling and stretching the dough to make 2 rounds about 25cm in diameter and 1–2cm thick. Make a small rim by pulling up the edges slightly.

4. Spread the passata over each pizza base, avoiding the rim. Leave to rest at room temperature for 15 minutes.

5. Scatter over the mozzarella and bake for 13 minutes. Lift each pizza onto a large plate and top with the avocado, tomatoes and rocket. Drizzle over a little balsamic glaze and serve immediately.

PIZZA CAKE WITH SEMI-DRIED TOMATOES, SPINACH AND GOAT'S CHEESE

Torta di Pizza con Pomodori Semi-Secchi, Spinaci e Formaggio di Capra

I came up with the idea for this recipe just by watching the way that people eat pizza. I noticed that they often take a slice and fold it, doubling it over, and I have tried to recreate that effect – so here we are!

SERVES 4

500g strong white flour,
   plus extra for dusting
1 x 7g sachet fast-action
   (easy blend) dried yeast
1 teaspoon salt
4 tablespoons extra virgin olive
   oil, plus extra for greasing
   and brushing
Sea salt flakes for sprinkling

For the filling
300g frozen spinach,
   defrosted and drained
200g semi-dried tomatoes
   in oil, drained
100g frozen peas, defrosted
4 tablespoons chopped fresh
   flat-leaf parsley
150g firm, mature goat's
   cheese, crumbled
Salt and freshly ground
   black pepper

1. Place the flour in a large bowl. Add the yeast to one side of the bowl and the salt to the other. Make a well in the centre and add the oil then gradually pour in 320ml warm water and mix together using the handle of a wooden spoon.

2. Knead the dough on a lightly floured surface for about 10 minutes or until smooth and elastic. Shape the dough into a round and place in an oiled bowl. Brush the top with oil and cover with cling film. Leave to rise in a warm place for about 1 hour or until doubled in size.

3. Preheat the oven to 210°C/gas mark 7. Grease a 25cm loose-bottomed cake tin and set aside. Squeeze as much liquid as you can out of the spinach, roughly chop, and place in a large bowl. Add the semi-dried tomatoes, peas and parsley and season with some salt and pepper. Mix well to combine.

4. Turn out the dough onto a lightly floured surface, knead 3 or 4 times and divide into two pieces: one consisting of two-thirds of the dough, the other one-third. Roll out the bigger piece 5cm larger than the tin and use it to line the bottom of the tin, bringing the excess up the side. Add the spinach mixture and sprinkle over the goat's cheese.

5. Roll out the remaining dough to the same size as the tin, brush the edges with a little water and place directly on the filling. Pinch the edges of the two pieces of dough together well to seal. Brush the top of the 'cake' with a little oil and sprinkle with the sea salt.

6. Bake for 35 minutes until risen and firm. Remove from the oven, place on a wire rack and let rest for 10 minutes. Remove from the tin, slice and serve warm.

FRIED PIZZA WITH MOZZARELLA AND FRESH BASIL

Pizza Margherita Fritta

Small fried pizzas are sometimes served as part of family meals in southern Italy. They're not for the calorie-conscious, but everyone needs a treat now and then – and this is a good one! You will need a 20–25cm frying pan with a well-fitted lid (or use foil if you don't have a lidded pan).

MAKES 8 SMALL, THIN PIZZAS

200g strong white flour, plus extra for dusting

1 x 7g sachet fast-action (easy blend) dried yeast

3/4 teaspoon salt

4 tablespoons extra virgin olive oil, plus extra for greasing

For the topping

2 tablespoons extra virgin olive oil, plus extra for drizzling

3 garlic cloves, peeled and thinly sliced

2 x 400g tins of chopped tomatoes

10 fresh basil leaves, plus a handful of shredded basil leaves to garnish

3 x 125g balls of mozzarella cheese, drained and cut into small pieces

Salt and freshly ground black pepper

1. Prepare the dough by placing the flour in a large bowl. Add the yeast to one side of the bowl and the salt to the other. Make a well in the centre and add 2 tablespoons olive oil then gradually pour in 140ml warm water and mix together using the handle of a wooden spoon.

2. Knead the dough on a lightly floured surface for about 5 minutes or until soft, smooth and elastic. Shape the dough into a round and place in a large oiled bowl. Brush the top with a little oil and cover with cling film. Leave to rest at room temperature for 30 minutes.

3. Meanwhile, make the topping. Heat the oil in a small saucepan over a medium heat. Add the garlic, and as it starts to sizzle add the tomatoes and whole basil leaves. Simmer gently for 10 minutes, stirring occasionally. Season and set aside.

4. Turn out the dough onto a lightly floured surface and knead 3 or 4 times. Divide the dough into 8 and form each piece into a ball. On a lightly floured surface, roll out the dough balls to make 8 very thin pizzas, each 20–25cm in diameter (they need to fit comfortably in the pan).

5. Heat the remaining 2 tablespoons of the oil in the frying pan over a medium heat. Slip one of the pizzas into the hot oil and fry for 2 minutes or until the underside is golden. Remove from the heat, turn over and spread 2 tablespoons of tomato sauce over the top. Scatter over some mozzarella and shredded basil and season. Drizzle over a little oil.

6. Place the frying pan back on the heat. Cover and cook for a further 2 minutes or until the mozzarella has melted. Remove, drain on kitchen paper and keep warm while you fry the remaining pizzas in the same way.

SUPER-SPICY CALZONE WITH SWEET PEPPERS AND OLIVES

Calzone Super-Piccante con Peperoni Dolci e Olive

I love calzone – there is something so exciting about them. Maybe it's because you can't see their contents, so the flavours take you by surprise. This calzone is filled with a piquant mixture of peppers, red onion and olives, which contrast with the creaminess of the ricotta, and the dried chillies give it a real kick.

MAKES 2

200g strong white flour,
    plus extra for dusting
1 x 7g sachet fast-action
    (easy blend) dried yeast
3/4 teaspoon salt
2 tablespoons extra virgin olive
    oil, plus extra for greasing
    and brushing
3 tablespoons chilli oil

For the filling
5 tablespoons extra virgin
    olive oil
1 red onion, peeled and
    thinly sliced
1 red pepper, deseeded and
    sliced into 5mm strips
1 yellow pepper, deseeded
    and sliced into 5mm strips
2 teaspoons dried chilli flakes
100g pitted Taggiasca olives,
    drained and halved
250g ricotta cheese
    (room temperature)
Salt

1. First make the filling. Heat the olive oil in a large frying pan over a medium heat. Add the onion, peppers, chilli flakes and salt and fry gently for 10 minutes, stirring occasionally. Add the olives, fry for 3 minutes and set aside.

2. Place the ricotta in a medium bowl and work with the back of a fork until smooth and easy to spread. Set aside.

3. Prepare the dough by placing the flour in a large bowl. Add the yeast to one side of the bowl and the salt to the other. Make a well in the centre and add the olive oil then gradually pour in 140ml warm water and mix together using the handle of a wooden spoon.

4. Knead the dough on a lightly floured surface for about 5 minutes or until soft, smooth and elastic. Shape into a round and place in a large oiled bowl. Brush the top with a little olive oil and cover with cling film. Rest at room temperature for 20 minutes. Brush 2 baking sheets with oil and set aside. Preheat the oven to 220°C/gas mark 7.

5. Turn out the dough onto a lightly floured surface and knead 3 or 4 times. Halve the dough and roll out each half directly onto an oiled baking sheet, rolling and stretching the dough to make 2 rounds about 25cm in diameter and 1–2cm thick. Make a small rim by pulling up the edges.

6. Spread the ricotta over half the surface of each pizza base, avoiding the rim, then spoon over the spicy pepper mixture. Fold over the empty half to enclose the filling. Pinch the edges to seal and crimp them by making tucks at regular intervals.

7. Brush the surface of each with chilli oil and bake for 14 minutes or until golden brown. Serve hot.

CALZONE WITH RICOTTA, PECORINO, MOZZARELLA, TOMATO AND PESTO

Calzone con Ricotta, Pecorino, Mozzarella, Pomodoro e Pesto

If you're a fan of cheese and tomato sandwiches, you'll love this calzone. For added flavour I've put rosemary into the dough and topped the calzone with basil pesto. You can use other cheeses if you prefer, but avoid strong kinds that can overpower the herbs.

MAKES 2

200g strong white flour,
   plus extra for dusting
1 x 7g sachet fast-action
   (easy blend) dried yeast
3/4 teaspoon salt
1 tablespoon chopped fresh
   rosemary
2 tablespoons extra virgin olive
   oil, plus extra for greasing

For the filling
250g ricotta cheese
   (room temperature)
50g pecorino cheese, grated
1 x 125g ball of mozzarella
   cheese, drained and
   thinly sliced
10 fresh yellow cherry
   tomatoes, halved
Salt and white pepper

For the topping
2 tablespoons shop-bought pesto
2 tablespoons extra virgin olive oil
2 tablespoons grated
   Parmesan cheese

1. First make the filling. Place the ricotta and pecorino in a medium bowl and season. Work with the back of a fork until smooth and easy to spread. Set aside.

2. Place the pesto for the topping in a small bowl, pour over the oil, stir to combine and set aside.

3. Prepare the dough by placing the flour in a large bowl. Add the yeast to one side of the bowl and the salt to the other. Scatter over the rosemary. Make a well in the centre and add the oil then gradually pour in 140ml warm water and mix together using the handle of a wooden spoon.

4. Knead the dough on a lightly floured surface for about 5 minutes or until soft, smooth and elastic. Shape into a round and place in a large oiled bowl. Brush the top with a little oil and cover with cling film. Leave to rest at room temperature for 20 minutes. Brush 2 baking sheets with oil and set aside. Preheat the oven to 220°C/gas mark 7.

5. Turn out the dough onto a lightly floured surface and knead 3 or 4 times. Halve the dough and roll out each half directly onto an oiled baking sheet, rolling and stretching the dough to make 2 rounds about 25cm in diameter and 1–2cm thick. Make a small rim by pulling up the edges.

6. Spread the ricotta mixture over half the surface of each pizza base, avoiding the rim, then arrange the slices of mozzarella and the tomatoes on top. Fold over the empty half to enclose the filling. Pinch the edges to seal and crimp them by making tucks at regular intervals.

7. Bake for 7 minutes then spread over the pesto and sprinkle over the Parmesan. Return to the oven for a further 7 minutes or until golden brown. Serve hot.

CAVOLO NERO, ROCKET AND ARTICHOKE TART WITH PROVOLONE CHEESE

Torta di Cavolo Nero, Rucola, Carciofi e Provolone

Also known as Tuscan black cabbage, cavolo nero has long been a popular autumn/winter vegetable in Italy. In recent years it has gained popularity in Britain and is now grown here. Similar to kale, cavolo nero has a strong, slightly bitter flavour and is a great source of vitamins A, C and K as well as iron and lutein. It is delicious baked in this tart with rocket, artichokes and provolone cheese.

SERVES 8

5 tablespoons olive oil
2 red onions, peeled and
    thinly sliced
1 tablespoon chopped fresh thyme
200g cavolo nero, tough
    central midribs removed
    and leaves shredded
200g rocket leaves,
    roughly chopped
8 chargrilled artichoke hearts
    in a jar, drained and halved
Butter for greasing
Flour for dusting
400g shop-bought shortcrust
    pastry
6 large eggs
150g provolone piccante
    cheese, grated
Salt and freshly ground
    black pepper

1. Heat the oil in a large frying pan or a wok over a high heat. Add the onions and thyme and fry for 4 minutes, stirring occasionally. Add the cavolo nero and rocket, season with salt and pepper and fry for 6 minutes, stirring occasionally. Tip in the artichokes and cook for 2 minutes. Check for seasoning and set aside.

2. Grease a 25cm loose-bottomed flan tin (ideally fluted) with butter. On a lightly floured surface, roll out the pastry and use it to line the tin. Chill in the freezer for 10 minutes. Meanwhile, preheat the oven to 190°C/gas mark 5.

3. 'Blind bake' the pastry case: prick the pastry base all over with a fork, line the bottom and sides with baking parchment and weigh it down with baking beans. Place on a baking sheet and bake for 10 minutes. Remove the beans and paper, return to the oven and bake for a further 3 minutes. Set aside to cool.

4. Lightly beat the eggs in a large bowl, add the provolone and season with salt and pepper. Stir to combine then add the vegetables and mix well. Turn the mixture into the cooled pastry case, spreading it out evenly.

5. Bake for 30 minutes or until the filling is golden and just set. Remove from the oven and allow the tart to cool in its tin for 10 minutes before serving.

ROASTED VEGETABLE PIE WITH LEMON ZEST AND FRESH ROSEMARY

Torta di Verdure al Forno con Scorza di Limone e Rosmarino

Savoury vegetable pies are a speciality of Liguria, in north-western Italy. The vegetables used vary according to the season. Here I have used roasted Mediterranean summer vegetables for the filling, but in winter you can replace them with butternut squash and root vegetables.

SERVES 8

8 tablespoons olive oil,
    plus extra for greasing
1 yellow pepper, deseeded
    and cut into 2cm cubes
1 red pepper, deseeded and
    cut into 2cm cubes
1 green pepper, deseeded
    and cut into 2cm cubes
2 courgettes, halved lengthways
    and cut into slices 1cm thick
1 large leek, halved lengthways
    and finely sliced
1 large red onion, peeled
    and finely sliced
2 tablespoons chopped
    fresh rosemary
2 large eggs
100ml double cream
100g freshly grated
    Parmesan cheese
Grated zest of 1 unwaxed lemon
2 x 320g sheets of shop-bought
    puff pastry (ready-rolled)
15 fresh cherry tomatoes
Salt and freshly ground
    black pepper

1. Preheat the oven to 200°C/gas mark 6. Grease a 25cm loose-bottomed flan tin (ideally fluted) with a little oil.

2. Place the peppers, courgettes, leek and onion in a large, shallow roasting tin, sprinkle over the rosemary and season with salt and pepper. Drizzle with the oil and toss together so the vegetables are well coated. Roast for 35 minutes, turning halfway through cooking. Check for seasoning and set aside to cool. Reduce the oven temperature to 180°C/gas mark 4.

3. In a medium bowl combine 1 egg with the cream, Parmesan and lemon zest, and season with salt and pepper. Set aside.

4. Carefully line the bottom and side of the flan tin with one puff pastry sheet, allowing a small overhang at the side. Arrange the cold roasted vegetables on top, scatter over the tomatoes and pour over the egg mixture. Cover the top of the tin with the remaining pastry sheet, press down the pastry edge to seal and trim off the excess using a small, sharp knife. Holding the knife horizontally and with its back to the edge of the pie, tap all around to secure the seal.

5. Beat the remaining egg in a small bowl and brush over the pie. Make a little slit in the centre of the pie lid, about 1–2cm long, to allow the steam to escape.

6. Place the tin on a baking sheet and bake for 30 minutes. Remove from the oven and let the pie rest in its tin for 5 minutes before serving.

SPINACH, ROCKET AND CHEESE PIE WITH A HINT OF CHILLI

Torta di Spinaci, Rucola e Formaggio con un Pizzico di Peperoncino

The crisp texture of the filo pastry in this recipe makes a striking contrast to the soft, creamy spinach filling. There is something elegant about filo pastry, and it's easy to use as there's no rolling out required. However, it does dry out very quickly and becomes brittle, so use it as soon as you've opened the packet, and keep it covered with a damp tea towel while you're building up the layers.

SERVES 8

350g frozen spinach,
    defrosted and drained
120ml olive oil, plus extra
    for greasing
1 red onion, peeled and finely
    chopped
$\frac{1}{2}$ teaspoon dried chilli flakes
100g rocket leaves,
    roughly chopped
$\frac{1}{4}$ teaspoon freshly grated
    nutmeg
150g ricotta cheese
120g mascarpone cheese
400g shop-bought filo pastry
Salt

1. Squeeze as much liquid as you can out of the spinach and roughly chop.

2. Heat 50ml of the oil in a large frying pan over a medium heat. Add the onion and fry gently for 5–10 minutes, stirring occasionally, until softened. Add the chilli flakes, spinach and rocket and cook for 2 minutes then season with a little salt and the nutmeg. Remove from the heat and stir in the ricotta and mascarpone. Set aside.

3. Preheat the oven to 190°C/gas mark 5. Grease a baking dish measuring about 30 x 23cm with a little oil. Place 1 sheet of filo pastry in the bottom of the dish, bringing it up and over the sides and allowing it to overhang the edges a little. Lightly brush with oil. Repeat with further filo sheets, overlapping them so the bottom and sides of the dish are completely covered. Continue in this way, layering filo sheets on top of each other and brushing with oil between them, until half the pastry is used.

4. Spread the spinach and rocket mixture evenly over the filo then cover the filling with the remaining filo sheets, layering and brushing oil between each sheet as before, until all the filo is used up.

5. Fold over the edges to seal. Brush the top with more oil and cut through the layers, right to the bottom of the dish, to make 8 rectangles.

6. Bake for 30 minutes or until the filo is golden brown and crispy. Leave to cool for 10 minutes then cut into the marked squares and lift from the dish. Serve warm.

RISOTTO
and other rice dishes

I often think it's amazing that although rice is just a small seed from a plant, it's such an important, even vital, part of our diet the world over. It is, of course, incredibly versatile; there are hundreds of thousands of recipes that can make this single humble ingredient taste completely different from one dish to the next. In Italy, rice is generally served as a first course rather than as an accompaniment. It is traditionally more common in the north, where the main rice-growing regions are to be found, than in central and southern Italy, where pasta is more prevalent.

The best-known Italian rice dish is undoubtedly risotto; wonderfully warming and filling – and requiring remarkably few ingredients – it's the perfect choice for a midweek supper. In this chapter I've included several risotto recipes, ringing the changes by using a selection of different vegetables. Some people are put off making risotto because they think they're going to be tied to the hob for pretty much the duration of the cooking; however, the steady stirring can actually be quite relaxing – and the end result of a delicious, creamy dish exploding with flavour is definitely worth it.

I've also included *arancini* (rice croquettes), which are great starters or snacks to have with drinks; a risotto timbale, which makes an impressive vegetarian main course; and a delicious, colourful rice salad. So let's get cooking!

Rice Croquettes Stuffed with Oozing
Mozzarella and Fresh Basil

Conical Rice Croquettes Stuffed with
Creamy Taleggio and Peas

Mamma's Neapolitan Rice Salad

Courgette and Roasted Pepper Risotto
with Provolone Cheese

Asparagus and Radicchio Risotto with Sage

Super-creamy Risotto with Prosecco,
Nutmeg and Spinach

Risotto Dome with Mushrooms

Risotto Timbale with Butternut Squash,
Artichokes and Aubergines

RICE CROQUETTES STUFFED WITH OOZING MOZZARELLA AND FRESH BASIL

Palle di Riso Ripiene di Mozzarella Fondente e Basilico

Rice croquettes, which are balls of cooked rice rolled in breadcrumbs and fried, are served in Italy as a starter, a snack or part of a buffet. These cheese-stuffed ones are a real winner in my house. You can substitute goat's cheese for the mozzarella if you prefer a stronger flavour.

MAKES 12

700ml vegetable stock
1 medium red onion,
    peeled and finely chopped
10 fresh basil leaves, shredded
320g Arborio or Carnaroli rice
250g tinned chopped tomatoes
1 large egg, lightly beaten
2 x 125g balls of mozzarella cheese,
    drained and cut into 12 cubes
150g dried fine breadcrumbs
About 1 litre sunflower
    oil for deep frying
Salt and freshly ground
    black pepper

1. Heat the vegetable stock in a large saucepan and add the onion and basil. Bring to the boil, add the rice and cook for 20 minutes, stirring occasionally. Drain and transfer the rice mixture to a large tray to cool. Stir in the tomatoes, beaten egg and some salt and pepper.

2. Form the mixture into 12 equal-sized balls, using wet hands to prevent the rice from sticking. Push a cube of mozzarella into the centre of each ball, mould the rice around to enclose and squeeze tightly between your hands to seal. Gently roll each ball in the breadcrumbs until evenly coated.

3. Heat a deep-fat fryer to 190°C, or heat the sunflower oil in a deep pan or wok until a cube of bread dropped in the hot oil sizzles and turns brown in 30 seconds. Make sure the oil is deep enough to completely cover the croquettes.

4. Deep fry the croquettes in batches for about 8 minutes or until golden brown and hot in the middle. Remove with a slotted spoon and drain on kitchen paper. Serve hot.

CONICAL RICE CROQUETTES STUFFED WITH CREAMY TALEGGIO AND PEAS

Arancini Ripieni di Taleggio Cremoso e Piselli

The fillings and shapes of rice croquettes vary – they're often spherical (their Italian name, arancini, means little oranges), but here I've made them more conical, as is typical in eastern Sicily. Some recipes, such as this one, start with a creamy risotto base, so it's a great way to use up leftover risotto. Don't overcook the risotto, or you'll end up with a stodgy mess.

MAKES 8

½ teaspoon saffron threads
1.3 litres hot vegetable stock
6 tablespoons olive oil
1 large onion, peeled and
    finely chopped
400g Arborio or Carnaroli rice
150ml dry white wine
100g salted butter (room
    temperature)
50g freshly grated Parmesan
    cheese
200g '00' grade pasta flour
150g frozen peas, defrosted
100g Taleggio cheese, rind
    removed and cut into 8 cubes
120g fresh fine breadcrumbs
About 1 litre sunflower oil
    for deep-frying
Salt and white pepper

1. First, make the risotto. Mix the saffron with 4 tablespoons of the hot stock in a small bowl and set aside to infuse. Meanwhile, heat the olive oil in a large, heavy-based saucepan over a medium heat. Add the onion and fry gently for 5 minutes, stirring, until softened but not browned. Add the rice and stir constantly for 3 minutes until the grains are coated and shiny.

2. Pour over the wine and simmer for about 1 minute. When it has evaporated, stir in the saffron mixture. Now start adding the hot stock, a ladleful or two at a time. Bring to a simmer and stir continuously until the liquid has been absorbed before adding the next ladleful. Repeat the process with the remaining stock until the rice is cooked but still has a slight bite. This will take 18–20 minutes and you may not need to use all the stock.

3. Remove the pan from the heat and stir in the butter and Parmesan for about 30 seconds. Season with some salt and pepper, cover and leave to rest for 15 minutes.

4. Meanwhile, prepare the batter. Put the flour in a large bowl. Add 300ml of cold water gradually, whisking between each addition until the batter is smooth and runny. Set aside.

5. When the risotto has cooled, tip it onto a clean work surface. Using dampened hands, press and squeeze the risotto for about 5 minutes until the mixture becomes denser and more compact. Shape the rice into 8 equal-sized balls.

6. Take one ball in the palm of your hand and flatten it a little. Place some peas and a cube of Taleggio in the centre, mould the rice around the filling to enclose and squeeze

tightly to seal. To make the conical shape, flatten one end and make the other more pointed. Repeat for all the balls. Carefully dip each cone in the batter and roll in the breadcrumbs until evenly coated.

7. Heat a deep-fat fryer to 190°C, or heat the sunflower oil in a deep pan or wok until a cube of bread dropped in the hot oil sizzles and turns brown in 30 seconds. Make sure the oil is deep enough to completely cover the croquettes.

8. Deep fry the croquettes in batches for about 8 minutes or until golden brown and hot in the middle. Remove with a slotted spoon and drain on kitchen paper. Serve hot.

MAMMA'S NEAPOLITAN RICE SALAD

Insalata di Riso Napoletana di Mia Mamma

Filled with many different vegetables and bursting with goodness, this rice salad is a great dish for buffets, packed lunches and picnics. As well as tasting great, it looks stunning as the colours are so vibrant. For a bit of kick, use chilli oil rather than lemon-flavoured olive oil – both work well.

SERVES 6

400g long-grain rice
100g frozen peas, defrosted
100g green beans, cut into
  2cm lengths
100g pitted giant green olives,
  drained and halved
100g pickled small gherkins,
  finely chopped
1 yellow pepper, deseeded
  and finely chopped
1 red pepper, deseeded and
  finely chopped
4 tablespoons mayonnaise
4 tablespoons extra virgin olive oil
10 fresh red cherry tomatoes,
  quartered
10 fresh yellow cherry tomatoes,
  quartered
8 boiled eggs, peeled and quartered
Lemon-flavoured olive oil
  for drizzling
Salt and freshly ground
  black pepper

1. Bring a large pan of salted water to the boil. Put in the rice and cook for about 12 minutes, stirring occasionally. Add the peas and beans and simmer for 3 minutes. Tip into a sieve placed over the sink, then rinse under cold running water for 1 minute. Drain thoroughly and put the rice into a large bowl. (Cooking times of the rice may vary depending on the brand.)

2. Add all the remaining ingredients, except the boiled eggs and lemon-flavoured olive oil, and stir gently. Season to taste with salt and pepper and cover with cling film. Chill in the fridge for 2 hours, stirring every 30 minutes, so all the flavours can combine.

3. About 20 minutes before serving, remove from the fridge. Transfer the rice salad to individual plates or a large platter and arrange the boiled eggs on top. Drizzle over a little lemon-flavoured olive oil and serve.

COURGETTE AND ROASTED PEPPER RISOTTO WITH PROVOLONE CHEESE

Risotto con Zucchine, Peperoni Grigliati e Provolone

In this recipe I use the classic combination of onions, peppers and courgettes but have added sharp, spicy cheese to give it greater piquancy – the flavours are absolutely incredible. You can, of course, roast your own peppers, but those sold in jars are a great time-saver and I think taste even better in this dish.

SERVES 4

100g salted butter
　(room temperature)
4 tablespoons olive oil
1 large red onion, peeled
　and finely chopped
4 tablespoons chopped
　fresh flat-leaf parsley
400g Arborio or Carnaroli rice
150ml dry white wine
1.3 litres hot vegetable stock
2 medium courgettes, cut into
　1cm cubes
300g mixed roasted or chargrilled
　peppers in a jar, drained and
　roughly sliced
80g freshly grated provolone
　piccante cheese
Salt and freshly ground
　black pepper

1. Heat half the butter with the oil in a large, heavy-based saucepan over a medium heat until the butter has melted. Add the onion and parsley and fry gently for 5 minutes, stirring, until the onions are softened but not browned. Add the rice and stir constantly for 3 minutes or until the grains are coated and shiny.

2. Pour over the wine and simmer for about 1 minute until it has evaporated. Add 2 ladlefuls of stock, bring to a simmer and stir until the stock is absorbed. Add the courgettes, then continue adding the stock in the same way, stirring and waiting for it to be absorbed before adding more.

3. After about 12 minutes stir in the peppers, then continue with the stirring and adding of the remaining stock for a further 3 minutes or until the rice is cooked but still has a slight bite. You may not need to use all the stock.

4. Remove the pan from the heat and add the remaining butter with the provolone, stirring for about 20 seconds. The risotto should not be too thick; you want it to ooze. Season with some salt and pepper and serve immediately.

ASPARAGUS AND RADICCHIO RISOTTO WITH SAGE

Risotto al Radicchio, Asparagi e Salvia

Many of you will have tried asparagus risotto, which is superb in its own right, but for those who love the bitter, spicy flavour of radicchio and the earthy aroma of sage, this is a heavenly combination. You can substitute chicory for the radicchio if you prefer, but the rich purple colour of the radicchio really does enhance this dish.

SERVES 4

100g salted butter
(room temperature)
4 tablespoons olive oil
1 large onion, peeled and
finely chopped
1 tablespoon shredded
fresh sage
400g Arborio or Carnaroli rice
150ml dry white wine
1.3 litres hot vegetable stock
1 small head of radicchio,
leaves finely shredded
12 fine asparagus spears,
woody ends removed and
cut into 2cm lengths
80g freshly grated pecorino
cheese
Salt and freshly ground
black pepper

1. Heat half the butter with the oil in a large, heavy-based saucepan over a medium heat until the butter has melted. Add the onion and sage and fry gently for 5 minutes, stirring, until the onion is softened but not browned. Add the rice and stir constantly for 3 minutes or until the grains are coated and shiny.

2. Pour over the wine and simmer for about 1 minute until it has evaporated. Add 2 ladlefuls of stock, bring to a simmer and stir until the stock is absorbed. Add the radicchio, then continue adding the stock in the same way, stirring and waiting for it to be absorbed before adding more.

3. After about 10 minutes stir in the asparagus, then continue stirring and adding the remaining stock for a further 7 minutes or until the rice is cooked but still has a slight bite. You may not need to use all the stock.

4. Remove the pan from the heat and add the remaining butter with the pecorino, stirring for about 20 seconds. Season with some salt and pepper and serve straightaway.

SUPER-CREAMY RISOTTO WITH PROSECCO, NUTMEG AND SPINACH

Risotto Super-Cremoso al Prosecco, Noce Moscata e Spinaci

Creamy and indulgent, this risotto is made with milk and Prosecco as well as the usual stock. Baby spinach leaves add flavour, texture and colour, and boost the vitamin content. Baby spinach is more delicate than mature spinach, with smaller leaves that are softer and have a milder flavour. They are superb for eating raw in salads or adding to many dishes at the end of cooking, as in this dish.

SERVES 4

1 litre full-fat milk
½ teaspoon nutmeg,
    freshly grated
100g salted butter
    (room temperature)
5 tablespoons olive oil
1 large onion, peeled and
    finely chopped
1 celery stick, finely chopped
400g Arborio or Carnaroli rice
200ml Prosecco
400ml hot vegetable stock
60g freshly grated
    Parmesan cheese
2 large handfuls of baby
    spinach leaves
Salt and white pepper

1. Pour the milk into a medium saucepan, add the nutmeg and bring just to the boil over a medium-high heat. Cover the pan, remove from the heat and set aside.

2. Heat half the butter with the oil in a large, heavy-based saucepan over a medium heat until the butter has melted. Add the onion and celery and fry gently for 5 minutes, stirring, until softened but not browned. Add the rice and stir constantly for 3 minutes or until the grains are coated and shiny.

3. Pour over the Prosecco and stir until it has evaporated. Gradually add the stock, a ladleful at a time. Bring to a simmer and stir continuously until it has been absorbed before adding the next ladleful. Once the stock is used up, add the warm milk. Cook, stirring occasionally, for a further 13 minutes or until the rice is cooked but still has a slight bite.

4. Take the pan off the heat and add the remaining butter, Parmesan and spinach, stirring for about 30 seconds. Season with salt and pepper and serve immediately.

RISOTTO DOME WITH MUSHROOMS

Bomba di Riso ai Funghi

If you have leftover risotto, this is a perfect way to create a new dish. If not, it's certainly worth starting from scratch. You can either make one large dome, as here, or small individual ones and serve them as a first course, reducing the cooking time to 10 minutes. Once you've mastered the technique you can be as creative as you wish with your vegetable choices, but for me mushrooms are definitely the winner.

SERVES 4

150g salted butter,
    plus extra for greasing
4 tablespoons olive oil
1 large red onion, peeled and
    finely chopped
1 tablespoon fresh thyme leaves
400g Arborio or Carnaroli rice
150ml dry white wine
1.3 litres hot vegetable stock
30g dried porcini mushrooms,
    soaked in hot water and drained
100g chestnut mushrooms, sliced
100g fresh ceps, sliced
80g freshly grated Parmesan
    cheese
100g fresh white breadcrumbs
Salt and freshly ground
    black pepper

1. Heat one-third of the butter with the oil in a large, heavy-based saucepan over a medium heat until the butter has melted. Add the onion and thyme and fry gently, stirring occasionally, for 5 minutes or until the onion is softened but not browned. Add the rice and stir constantly for 3 minutes or until the grains are coated and shiny.

2. Pour over the wine and simmer for about 1 minute or until it has evaporated. Add 2 ladlefuls of stock, bring to a simmer and stir until the stock is absorbed. Add all the mushrooms. Continue adding the remaining stock in the same way, stirring and waiting for it to be absorbed before adding more, until the rice is cooked but still has a slight bite. This will take 15–17 minutes after adding the mushrooms, and you may not need to use all the stock.

3. Take the pan off the heat and add one-third of the butter with the Parmesan, stirring for about 20 seconds. Season with some salt and pepper, cover and set aside to cool.

4. Preheat the oven to 190°C/gas mark 5. Grease a 2-litre ovenproof glass bowl with butter and sprinkle in a handful of the breadcrumbs to coat the sides and bottom. Tip out any excess breadcrumbs and reserve.

5. Spoon the cooled risotto into the bowl and sprinkle with all the remaining breadcrumbs. Cut the remaining butter into small pieces and dot over the top. Bake for 20 minutes or until golden brown.

6. Remove from the oven and let stand for 5 minutes. Run a knife around the edge of the bowl to loosen the sides. Now turn out the risotto dome onto a large, flat serving plate: place the plate upside down over the bowl then carefully turn them over together. Gently ease the bowl off the risotto dome and serve.

RISOTTO TIMBALE WITH BUTTERNUT SQUASH, ARTICHOKES AND AUBERGINES

Timballo di Risotto con Zucca, Carciofi e Melanzane

You need to devote time to making this recipe. Pour yourself a drink and stay by your pan – I promise, it will be worth it! If you're serving this at a dinner party, it will be an impressive new dish for guests to try. You may not think it will feed six, but because this risotto is so packed with wholesome vegetables and can be extremely filling, I really feel you will be full with one wedge. Serve with roasted tomatoes.

SERVES 6

5 tablespoons olive oil
1 large red onion, peeled
   and finely chopped
350g Arborio or Carnaroli rice
2 tablespoons chopped
   fresh rosemary
150ml dry white wine
250g butternut squash, deseeded,
   peeled and cut into 1cm cubes
10 artichoke hearts in oil,
   drained and quartered
1.2 litres hot vegetable stock
50g salted butter, plus extra
   for greasing
60g freshly grated Parmesan
   cheese
100g plain flour
2 aubergines, sliced into rounds
   5mm thick
2–4 tablespoons sunflower oil
Salt and freshly ground
   black pepper

1. Heat the olive oil in a large, heavy-based saucepan over a medium heat. Add the onion and fry gently for about 5 minutes, stirring, until softened but not browned. Add the rice and rosemary and stir constantly for 3 minutes or until the grains are coated and shiny.

2. Pour over the wine and simmer for about 1 minute until it has evaporated. Add the squash and half the artichokes. Add 2 ladlefuls of stock, bring to a simmer and stir until the stock is absorbed. Continue adding the stock in the same way, stirring and waiting for it to be absorbed before adding more.

3. After about 12 minutes stir in the remaining artichokes, then continue to stir and add the remaining stock for a further 3 minutes or until the rice is cooked but still has a slight bite. You may not need to use all the stock.

4. Take the pan off the heat and add the butter and Parmesan, stirring for about 30 seconds. Season with salt and pepper and set aside.

5. Preheat the oven to 180°C/gas mark 4. Grease a round ovenproof dish, with a diameter of about 26cm and at least 5–7cm deep, with butter. Put the flour on a large plate and dip the aubergine rounds into the flour to coat evenly on both sides. Tap off the excess.

6. Heat 1 tablespoon of the sunflower oil in a large frying pan and place over a medium heat. Add a single layer of aubergine slices and fry for 3–4 minutes on each side

until golden. Lift out with a slotted spoon, drain on kitchen paper and season with a little salt. Fry the remaining slices in batches, adding more oil if necessary.

7. Line the bottom and sides of the greased dish with overlapping aubergine slices, allowing them to overhang the sides of the dish. Carefully spoon the risotto into the dish. Lay the remaining aubergine slices over the top and fold over the overhanging slices so the risotto is completely enclosed. Bake for 30 minutes.

8. Remove from the oven and leave to rest for 15 minutes. To invert the timbale, hold a large wooden chopping board over the top of the dish and turn it over quickly. Leave on the chopping board and cut into wedges. Serve warm.

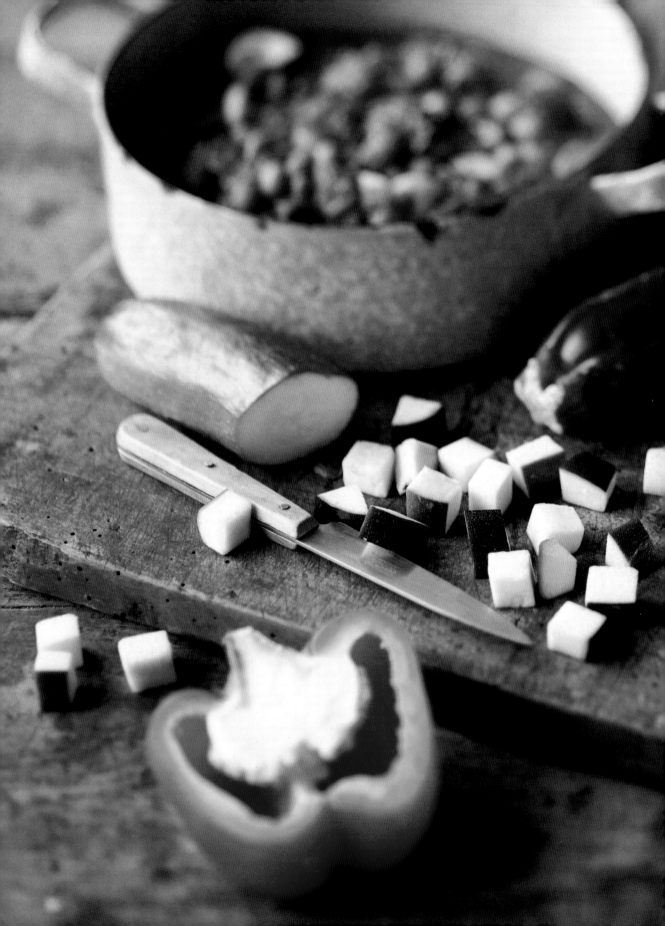

STEWS
AND
BAKES

This chapter is dedicated to all those busy people who work hard throughout the day, whether in an office or running around after children. You can prepare your meal ahead – in the morning or even the day before in some cases – and just cook or heat it through when ready. In the meantime, you can relax and have a bath or a glass of wine and just wait for that perfect 'welcome home' meal.

The ingredients and flavour combinations in all these dishes are good just as they are, but if you're making one of the stews feel free to add any vegetables or pulses you wish and be as creative as you like. However, when it comes to the bakes you will need to be a little more careful, as they are generally less forgiving than stews; some ingredients take longer to cook or produce more water than others, which might adversely affect the textures and consistency of the dish as a whole.

Whichever recipe you choose from this chapter, I am sure that you will love it – all the dishes are firm favourites in the D'Acampo household. And don't wait until the cold, dark winter months to try them; they are delicious at any time of year.

Roast Pumpkin with Gorgonzola and Walnuts

Summer Vegetable Stew with Cheesy Dumplings

Four-bean Stew with Soured Cream and Chives

Pearl Barley and Curly Kale Stew with Sage

Celeriac, Sweet Potato and Rosemary Gratin

Roasted Vegetable Ratatouille

Whole Roasted Cauliflower with Cheese Sauce

Aubergine Parmigiana

Lentil and Mushroom 'Meatballs'
with Herb Salsa

ROAST PUMPKIN WITH GORGONZOLA AND WALNUTS

Zucca al Forno con Gorgonzola e Noci

In autumn, pumpkins are in every supermarket, ready to be carved for Hallowe'en, so I recommend you pick up an extra one and try this recipe. Alternatively, butternut squash or sweet potatoes will do just as well. Serve with a crispy salad on the side and plenty of fresh bread.

SERVES 4

1 small pumpkin, about 1.5kg, halved, deseeded and peeled
5 garlic cloves
1 teaspoon dried chilli flakes
1/4 teaspoon freshly grated nutmeg
4 tablespoons olive oil
50g walnut halves, roughly chopped
150g Gorgonzola cheese, crumbled
Salt

1. Preheat the oven to 190°C/gas mark 5. Cut each pumpkin half into 6 wedges and place in a large, shallow roasting tin.

2. Lightly crush the garlic cloves with the back of a knife and add to the tin. Sprinkle over the chilli flakes, nutmeg and some salt and drizzle over the oil. Toss together so everything is coated in the oil. Roast for 30 minutes.

3. Remove the tin from the oven and scatter over the walnuts (do not stir them in). Return to the oven for 5 minutes to lightly toast the nuts. Spoon the mixture onto a large serving platter, scatter over the Gorgonzola and serve immediately.

SUMMER VEGETABLE STEW WITH CHEESY DUMPLINGS

Stufatino di Verdure Estive con Gnocchi al Formaggio

Stews aren't always winter fare. Summer vegetables can make delicious light casseroles that are ready in minutes rather than hours, and tasty dumplings turn them into substantial one-pot meals.

SERVES 4

3 tablespoons olive oil
25g salted butter
8 small shallots, peeled
1 tablespoon plain flour
100ml dry white wine
200ml hot vegetable stock
200ml double cream
1 tablespoon chopped
    fresh tarragon
200g baby carrots
200g baby courgettes,
    halved lengthways
130g baby leeks
150g asparagus spears,
    woody ends removed and
    cut into 4cm lengths
200g frozen peas, defrosted
Chopped fresh flat-leaf parsley
    to garnish

For the dumplings
100g self-raising flour
50g salted butter (room
    temperature)
50g freshly grated Parmesan
    cheese
1 teaspoon dried oregano
2 tablespoons chopped fresh
    flat-leaf parsley
Salt and freshly ground
    black pepper

1. First make the dumpling mixture. Place the flour in a large bowl. Rub the butter into the flour using your fingertips until the mixture resembles fine breadcrumbs. Stir in the Parmesan, oregano and parsley and season with a little salt and lots of black pepper. Set aside.

2. Heat the oil and butter in a large, heavy-based saucepan over a medium heat. Add the shallots and fry gently for 5 minutes or until they start to take on some colour. Stir in the plain flour and cook for 1 minute.

3. Increase the heat to high and deglaze the pan with the wine. Reduce the heat slightly to medium high and pour in the stock, stirring continuously to prevent lumps from forming. Once all the stock has been added, bring to the boil and stir in the cream, tarragon and some salt and pepper. Simmer for 2 minutes.

4. Meanwhile, add 2 tablespoons of cold water to the dumpling mix and bring together to form a soft but not sticky dough. You may need to add a little more water. Divide the dough into 4 equal-sized pieces then divide each piece into 5 and roll into small balls using floured hands. Set aside.

5. Add the carrots, courgettes and leeks to the saucepan and stir. Place the dumplings on top of the vegetables. Cover and cook for 10 minutes over a medium heat.

6. Carefully add the asparagus and peas, ensuring the dumplings do not sink into the liquid. Cover again and cook for a further 5 minutes or until the vegetables are cooked and the dumplings have puffed up and are soft. Check the seasoning one last time and garnish with the parsley before serving.

FOUR-BEAN STEW WITH SOURED CREAM AND CHIVES

Stufato di Fagioli Misti con Panna Acida ed Erba Cipollina

Stufato is one of my favourite ways to cook beans – it's so simple, satisfying and full of flavour. Beans are packed with goodness, being rich in protein, carbohydrates and fibre. I use tinned ones for this recipe, as they save you hours of soaking and cooking, and work perfectly well. You can also add a few chickpeas if you fancy. Serve on a bed of plain boiled rice.

SERVES 4

4 tablespoons olive oil
1 large onion, peeled and
    finely chopped
2 celery sticks, finely chopped
1 fresh, medium-hot red chilli,
    deseeded and finely chopped
1 tablespoon tomato purée
100ml dry white wine
400g fresh red cherry
    tomatoes, halved
Pinch of saffron threads
200ml hot vegetable stock
1 x 400g tin of borlotti beans,
    rinsed and drained
1x 400g tin of cannellini beans,
    rinsed and drained
1 x 400g tin of kidney beans,
    rinsed and drained
100g green beans, cut into
    2cm lengths
4 tablespoons soured cream
1 tablespoon chopped
    fresh chives
Salt and freshly ground
    black pepper

1. Heat the oil in a large saucepan over a medium heat. Add the onion, celery and chilli and fry gently for 10 minutes, stirring occasionally. Add the tomato purée and fry for 1 minute.

2. Increase the heat to high, pour in the wine and cook for 2 minutes to allow the alcohol from the wine to evaporate. Add the tomatoes and saffron and cook for 3 minutes.

3. Pour in the stock and bring to a simmer. Reduce the heat to medium, add all the beans and cook for 5 minutes or until the tinned beans are warmed through and the green beans are cooked but still al dente. Season with salt.

4. Put the soured cream in a small bowl and season with salt and pepper. Top each portion with the soured cream and chives.

PEARL BARLEY AND CURLY KALE STEW WITH SAGE

Stufato di Orzo Perlato, Cavolo Riccio e Salvia

Kale is a superfood. It is full of vitamins, including A, C and K, and is high in fibre and a rich source of protein. It's quite a robust vegetable, so you can cook it for a long time, but in this recipe I have added it right at the end to retain as many nutrients as possible. Serve with crusty bread to mop up the juices.

SERVES 4

4 tablespoons olive oil
2 carrots, peeled and
   very finely diced
2 celery sticks, finely diced
2 leeks, finely sliced
2 garlic cloves, crushed
1 tablespoon chopped
   fresh sage
300g pearl barley, rinsed
   and drained
1.5 litres hot vegetable stock
100g curly kale, tough central
   midribs removed and leaves
   shredded
25g salted butter
50g freshly grated pecorino
   cheese
Salt and freshly ground
   black pepper

1. Heat the oil in a large saucepan over a medium heat. Add the carrots, celery and leeks and fry gently for 15 minutes or until softened, stirring occasionally.

2. Add the garlic and sage and cook for about 1 minute then stir in the pearl barley and stock. Bring to the boil over a high heat, then reduce the heat, cover and simmer gently for 20 minutes, stirring occasionally.

3. Add the kale and cook for 5 minutes until wilted then stir in the butter. Check the consistency, adding a little more stock if needed, and season with salt and pepper. Pour into warm bowls, scatter over the pecorino and serve straightaway.

CELERIAC, SWEET POTATO AND ROSEMARY GRATIN

Gratinato di Sedano Rapa, Patata Dolce e Rosmarino

Celeriac is such an under-used vegetable, yet it is so versatile. You can mash, roast and bake it, or eat it raw in salads. It's good for you too, being a rich source of vitamin K and high in fibre. In this dish it's baked with sweet potatoes and a creamy sauce and topped with herby breadcrumbs to give a crispy crust. If you can't find celeriac, substitute it with 500g white potatoes, as sweet potatoes on their own would be far too sweet and rich.

SERVES 8

400ml double cream
400ml full-fat milk
2 garlic cloves, peeled and crushed
1 tablespoon wholegrain mustard
1 large celeriac, peeled, quartered
  and thinly sliced
500g sweet potatoes,
  peeled and thinly sliced
40g fresh breadcrumbs
25g salted butter, melted
1 tablespoon chopped
  fresh rosemary
Salt and white pepper

1. Preheat the oven to 180°C/gas mark 4. Heat the cream, milk and garlic in a medium saucepan over a high heat. Bring to the boil then remove from the heat. Leave to rest for 10 minutes then stir in the mustard.

2. Pour a little of the cream mixture into the bottom of a baking dish measuring about 20 x 20cm. Place a layer of the celeriac on top, season with salt and pepper, pour over a little more of the cream then a layer of sweet potato. Repeat the process twice more finishing with the cream. Bake for 45 minutes.

3. Meanwhile, combine the breadcrumbs, melted butter, rosemary and lots of pepper in a bowl.

4. Remove the baking dish from the oven and sprinkle over the breadcrumb mixture. Return to the oven for a further 30 minutes or until golden. Leave to rest for 5 minutes at room temperature before serving.

ROASTED VEGETABLE RATATOUILLE

Ratatouille di Verdure al Forno

This is how my auntie Clara taught me to make ratatouille, as she believed roasting the vegetables first gives the dish a sweeter, more intense flavour. Serve with warm, crusty bread.

SERVES 6–8

1 red pepper, deseeded and
   cut into 2cm chunks
1 yellow pepper, deseeded
   and cut into 2cm chunks
1 orange pepper, deseeded
   and cut into 2cm chunks
3 courgettes, sliced into rounds
   2cm thick
2 red onions, peeled and
   each cut into 8 wedges
2 medium aubergines,
   cut into 2cm chunks
6 large fresh plum tomatoes,
   each cut into 8 pieces
6 tablespoons olive oil
2 tablespoons balsamic vinegar
1 tablespoon fresh thyme leaves
Salt and freshly ground
   black pepper

For the sauce
2 tablespoons extra virgin olive
   oil, plus extra for drizzling
1 fresh, large, medium-hot red
   chilli, deseeded and
   finely chopped
2 garlic cloves, peeled and sliced
700ml passata (sieved tomatoes)
10 fresh basil leaves
   (5 shredded, 5 whole)
50g Parmesan cheese shavings

1. Preheat the oven to 180°C/gas mark 4. Place all the vegetables in a large, shallow roasting tin. Drizzle over the oil and vinegar and sprinkle over the thyme, salt and pepper. Toss everything together to combine and roast for 1 hour, turning all the vegetables halfway through the roasting time.

2. Meanwhile, make the sauce. Heat the oil in a medium saucepan over a medium heat. Add the chilli and garlic and fry for 30 seconds then pour in the passata and add the shredded basil and salt. Simmer gently for 10 minutes, stirring occasionally.

3. Tip the roasted vegetables into the sauce. Check the seasoning once more and stir gently to combine.

4. Spoon the ratatouille onto a large serving platter, garnish with the whole basil leaves, scatter over the Parmesan and drizzle over a little oil. Serve immediately.

WHOLE ROASTED CAULIFLOWER WITH CHEESE SAUCE

Cavolfiore al Forno con Besciamella al Formaggio

A spicy Italian version of cauliflower cheese, here the cauliflower is roasted whole and topped with the cheese sauce. It's a great way to use up any small pieces of cheese you may have in the back of the fridge. Serve with crusty bread to mop up any leftover sauce.

SERVES 2–4

1 cauliflower, leaves removed
1 tablespoon black peppercorns
1 tablespoon salt
3 sprigs of fresh rosemary
50g freshly grated Parmesan
    cheese
1 teaspoon dried chilli flakes
1 egg, lightly beaten and seasoned
    with salt and pepper
Olive oil for greasing

For the cheese sauce
40g salted butter
30g plain flour
600ml full-fat milk
100g freshly grated Cheddar
    cheese
50g freshly grated Parmesan
    cheese
1 teaspoon English mustard
5 spring onions, chopped
1 tablespoon chopped
    fresh flat-leaf parsley
Salt

1. Place the whole cauliflower in a large pan. Cover with water and add the peppercorns, salt and rosemary. Bring to the boil over a high heat then reduce the heat and simmer for 20 minutes, turning halfway through cooking, until almost tender. Drain and discard the flavourings. Transfer the cauliflower to a wire rack for 15 minutes. Preheat the oven to 200°C/gas mark 6.

2. Combine the Parmesan and chilli flakes on a large plate. Brush the cauliflower with the beaten egg then roll it in the Parmesan and chilli mixture until evenly coated. Place in an oiled roasting tin and roast for 18 minutes until golden brown.

3. Meanwhile, make the cheese sauce. Melt the butter in a medium saucepan over a medium heat until foaming. Add the flour and cook for 1–2 minutes until pale golden, stirring continuously. Now start adding the milk a little at a time, whisking constantly and waiting for it to be incorporated before adding more. Bring to the boil then reduce the heat and simmer gently for 5–10 minutes, whisking occasionally, until thickened and smooth.

4. Remove the pan from the heat and stir in the cheeses until melted. Mix in the mustard, spring onions and parsley and season with salt.

5. Remove the cauliflower from the oven and place on a large serving platter. Pour over the cheese sauce.

AUBERGINE PARMIGIANA

Melanzane alla Parmigiana

Aubergine Parmigiana is one of Italy's most well-known baked dishes. Some say it comes from the north of Italy, because of the Parmesan cheese, while others place it firmly in the south due to the aubergines and tomatoes. Wherever it comes from, it's a family favourite and I love it. Serve with lots of warm bread on the side.

SERVES 6

3 large aubergines, sliced
  into rounds 1cm thick
4 tablespoons olive oil,
  plus extra for drizzling
70g freshly grated Parmesan
  cheese for the layers,
  plus 30g for the topping
1 x 125g ball of mozzarella
  cheese, torn into
  small pieces
20g dried breadcrumbs

For the tomato sauce
2 tablespoons olive oil
2 garlic cloves, peeled and
  finely sliced
2 x 400g tins of chopped
  tomatoes
15 fresh basil leaves
Salt and freshly ground
  black pepper

1. First make the tomato sauce. Heat the oil in a medium saucepan over a medium heat. Add the garlic, and as soon as it starts to sizzle tip in the tomatoes then season with some salt and pepper. Simmer gently for 15 minutes, stirring occasionally. Add the basil and check again for seasoning. Set aside.

2. Preheat a ridged cast-iron chargrill pan over a high heat for 5–10 minutes. Brush the aubergines with the oil and chargrill in batches, cooking both sides until soft and the markings from the ridged pan have become a dark golden colour (about 5–6 minutes in total). Set aside.

3. Preheat the oven to 180°C/gas mark 4. Spread a thin layer of the tomato sauce in a baking dish measuring about 25 x 12cm. Sprinkle over a little Parmesan, cover with a layer of aubergines and season with salt and pepper. Continue layering twice more, finishing with the sauce.

4. Scatter over the mozzarella. Combine the breadcrumbs with the 30g Parmesan for the topping and drizzle over a little olive oil.

5. Bake for about 40 minutes or until golden. Switch off the oven and leave to rest inside the oven with the door closed for 20 minutes. Serve warm.

LENTIL AND MUSHROOM 'MEATBALLS' WITH HERB SALSA

Polpette di Lenticchie e Funghi con Salsa alle Erbe

These lentil 'meatballs' are really versatile. They can be served with the salsa for a first course, snack or light lunch, or with pasta and polenta for a more substantial meal.

SERVES 6

200g dried green lentils,
   rinsed and drained
1 litre vegetable stock
4 tablespoons olive oil,
   plus extra for greasing
1 carrot, peeled and grated
1 small onion, peeled and grated
2 tablespoons tomato purée
150g chestnut mushrooms,
   finely chopped
1 tablespoon fresh thyme leaves
2 medium eggs, lightly beaten
40g fresh breadcrumbs
40g freshly grated Parmesan
   cheese
3 tablespoons chopped
   fresh flat-leaf parsley
Salt and freshly ground
   black pepper

For the salsa
1 garlic clove, chopped
Handful (about 40g) of chopped
   fresh flat-leaf parsley
20 fresh mint leaves, chopped
Handful (about 40g) of shredded
   fresh basil leaves
1 tablespoon capers, drained
4 baby gherkins, chopped
2 tablespoons red wine vinegar
2 teaspoons Dijon mustard
4 tablespoons extra virgin olive oil

1. Place the lentils in a medium saucepan with the stock and bring to the boil over a high heat. Reduce the heat and simmer gently for about 25 minutes or until the lentils are tender but still retain their bite. Drain and set aside.

2. Heat 1 tablespoon of the olive oil in a large frying pan over a medium heat. Add the carrot and onion and fry gently for about 5–10 minutes or until softened, stirring occasionally. Stir in the tomato purée and cook for about 1 minute then add the mushrooms and thyme. Fry for 15 minutes until all the liquid from the mushrooms has evaporated then season with salt and pepper. Remove from the heat and leave to cool.

3. Place the cooked lentils and mushroom mixture in a large bowl with the beaten eggs, breadcrumbs, Parmesan, parsley and some salt and pepper. Stir thoroughly to combine. Cover with cling film and chill in the fridge for about 1 hour. Preheat the oven to 180°C/gas mark 4. Grease a baking sheet with a little oil.

4. Using dampened hands, shape the lentil mixture into 12 even-sized balls, each about the size of a golf ball. Place on the greased baking sheet, drizzle with the remaining olive oil and bake for about 25–30 minutes.

5. Meanwhile, make the salsa. Put the garlic, herbs, capers and gherkins in a large bowl. Add the vinegar and mustard, then gradually whisk in the extra virgin olive oil. Season with some salt and pepper.

6. When the lentil balls are golden and crispy, remove the baking sheet from the oven and let stand for 5 minutes. Serve with the salsa on the side.

SOUPS

I'm a big fan of soups. They're the best way to pack a great number of vegetables into one dish and they're full of goodness. Lighter, more delicate soups make an appetising first course, while heartier ones (in Italy, often thickened with pasta, rice or pearl barley) can be sustaining enough to amount to a meal in themselves. Many Italian soups are accompanied by plenty of freshly grated Parmesan or pecorino cheese, either stirred in or served separately on the side.

It's a running joke in our family that whenever anyone seems to be getting a cold or starts showing the slightest hint of illness, a soup is made. I'll never forget the time when I was about 14 years old and had a slightly runny nose; my mother made me a chunky minestrone soup, which I had to eat sitting on the beach in a 40-degree heatwave, while all my friends were enjoying ice-cream. You might think I'd have been embarrassed, but on the contrary – my friends all begged me to let them have some of my soup! I think I realised then that soup is something to be enjoyed at any time of year. Having said that, though, it's true that some are strictly seasonal – for instance, in this chapter you'll find a chilled vegetable soup, which is perfect in the heat of the summer.

Soups are quick, easy and rewarding to make. The difficulty will be deciding which one of these delicious soups you should try first!

Roasted Root Vegetable Soup with
Caramelised Onion Topping

Tomato and Borlotti Bean Soup
with Cheesy Ciabatta

The D'Acampo Family's Minestrone

Winter Vegetable and Spinach Soup

Traditional Italian Peasant's Soup

Chilled Spicy Summer Soup with Tomatoes,
Avocado and Sweetcorn

Perfect Autumn Soup with Butternut Squash,
Orange and Fresh Ginger

Spicy Pumpkin and Pasta Soup

Pearl Barley, Fennel and Cannellini Bean Soup
with Cheesy Panini

ROASTED ROOT VEGETABLE SOUP WITH CARAMELISED ONION TOPPING

Vellutata di Verdure Guarnita con Cipolle Fritte

Thick, creamy and packed with root vegetables, this soup makes excellent winter fuel. Don't worry if the edges of the vegetables turn brown in the oven – they will intensify the flavour, which becomes almost smoky and sweet. The caramelised onion topping provides an exciting contrast of texture, flavour and colour.

SERVES 4

300g butternut squash, deseeded, peeled and cut into 1cm chunks
1 large carrot, peeled and sliced into rounds
1 small parsnip, peeled and cut into 1cm chunks
1/2 small swede, peeled and cut into 1cm chunks
1 leek, sliced into rounds
1/2 red onion, peeled and cut into 1cm chunks
1 small turnip, peeled and cut into 1cm chunks
1 small potato, peeled and cut into 1cm chunks
40ml olive oil
2 bay leaves
800ml hot vegetable stock
250ml full-fat milk
100g mascarpone cheese
Salt and white pepper

For the topping
3 teaspoons olive oil
1/2 red onion, peeled and thinly sliced

1. Preheat the oven to 200°C/gas mark 6. Put all the prepared vegetables in a large, shallow roasting tin. Pour over the oil, season with salt and pepper and toss together so all the vegetables are coated in the oil. Tuck the bay leaves under the vegetables to prevent burning. Roast for 45 minutes, turning the vegetables halfway through.

2. Meanwhile, make the topping. Heat the oil in a small frying pan over a medium-low heat. Add the onion and fry for 10–15 minutes, stirring only very occasionally; if you stir too much, the onions will not caramelise properly.

3. Remove the roasting tin from the oven and discard the bay leaves. Tip the vegetables into a large saucepan and pour over the stock and milk. Bring to the boil over a high heat then reduce the heat and simmer for 10 minutes.

4. Using a blender or food processor, blitz the soup until smooth. Return to the heat and bring to a simmer, then reduce the heat to low and stir in the mascarpone (blitz again if using a hand-held blender). Season with salt and pepper. Ladle the soup into warm bowls and top with the caramelised onions.

TOMATO AND BORLOTTI BEAN SOUP WITH CHEESY CIABATTA

Zuppa di Pomodori e Borlotti con Ciabatta al Formaggio

This rich, chunky soup served with cheesy ciabatta is a meal in itself. Borlotti beans are large and plump, with a creamy, meaty texture. If you prefer, you can substitute them with lentils or the smaller, white cannellini beans.

SERVES 6

4 tablespoons olive oil
2 large red onions, peeled
   and roughly chopped
2 x 400g tins of chopped tomatoes
2 tablespoons sun-dried
   tomato paste
2 teaspoons paprika
2 teaspoons sugar
1.2 litres hot vegetable stock
1 tablespoon cornflour
1 tablespoon balsamic vinegar
1 x 400g tin of borlotti beans,
   rinsed and drained
3 tablespoons chopped
   fresh flat-leaf parsley
Salt and freshly ground
   black pepper

For the cheesy ciabatta
100g salted butter (room
   temperature)
2 tablespoons chopped
   fresh flat-leaf parsley
2 x 300g ciabatta loaves
150g Asiago cheese, grated

1. Preheat the oven to 180°C/gas mark 4. Heat the oil in a large saucepan over a medium heat. Add the onions and fry gently for 5–10 minutes, stirring occasionally.

2. Stir in the tomatoes, sun-dried tomato paste, paprika and sugar. Pour in the stock, bring to the boil over a high heat then reduce the heat and simmer gently for 15 minutes, stirring occasionally.

3. Put the cornflour in a small bowl with the vinegar and mix to a paste. Stir into the soup together with the beans and simmer for 5 minutes. Add the parsley, season with salt and pepper and cook for a further 5 minutes or until the soup thickens slightly.

4. Meanwhile, make the cheesy ciabatta. Put the butter in a small bowl with the parsley and beat together using a small wooden spoon. Carefully cut 8 vertical slits in each ciabatta loaf, without cutting right through. Spread parsley butter between the slits, then stuff in some Asiago. Wrap the loaves individually in foil, place them direct on the oven shelf and bake for 15 minutes or until golden and crunchy and the cheese has melted.

5. Ladle the soup into warm bowls or cups and serve immediately with the cheesy ciabatta on the side.

THE D'ACAMPO FAMILY'S MINESTRONE

Minestrone della Famiglia D'Acampo

Minestrone recipes differ across Italy; most include pasta and beans, as well as tomatoes, carrots, celery and onions (or leeks), but the other ingredients are variable. This recipe is my own family's favourite. You can make this soup the day before it's needed and reheat it. In fact, I think it tastes even better the second day, as the flavours have had more time to mingle.

SERVES 6

4 tablespoons extra virgin olive oil
1 leek, thinly sliced
2 medium carrots, peeled and
    thinly sliced
1 large courgette, halved
    lengthways and roughly sliced
2 celery sticks, roughly sliced
120g green beans, cut into
    2cm lengths
1.5 litres hot vegetable stock
1 x 400g tin of chopped tomatoes
1 tablespoon tomato purée
Small handful (about 25g) of
    shredded fresh basil leaves
3 tablespoons fresh thyme leaves
1 x 400g tin of cannellini beans,
    rinsed and drained
3 tablespoons chopped
    fresh flat-leaf parsley
75g mini pasta shapes
80g freshly grated Parmesan
    cheese
Salt and freshly ground
    black pepper

1. Heat the oil in a large saucepan over a medium heat. Add the leek, carrots, courgette, celery and green beans and fry gently for 15 minutes, stirring occasionally.

2. Pour in the stock and stir in the tomatoes, tomato purée, basil, thyme, and some salt and pepper. Bring to the boil over a high heat then reduce the heat, half-cover with a lid and simmer gently for 35 minutes, stirring occasionally.

3. Add the cannellini beans and parsley and cook for 5 minutes, then add the pasta and cook for about 5 minutes or until al dente. Ladle into warm bowls and sprinkle over the freshly grated Parmesan.

WINTER VEGETABLE AND SPINACH SOUP

Zuppa di Verdure Invernali e Spinaci

This hearty winter vegetable soup is ideal for finishing off all the odd vegetables in the fridge. Substitutions work well here – experiment and the flavour changes will be your reward. I prefer this soup chunky, but it can be blended very easily to give a silky-smooth texture.

SERVES 6

4 tablespoons olive oil
1 leek, thinly sliced
1 onion, peeled and finely chopped
1 celery stick, roughly diced
1 small waxy potato, peeled
    and roughly diced
1 parsnip, peeled and
    roughly diced
1/2 fennel bulb, cored and
    thinly sliced
1 carrot, peeled and roughly diced
1.2 litres hot vegetable stock
2 tablespoons tomato purée
200g fresh spinach, shredded
2 spring onions, finely chopped
6 tablespoons chopped fresh
    oregano leaves
Salt and freshly ground
    black pepper

1. Heat the oil in a medium saucepan over a medium heat. Add the leek, onion, celery, potato, parsnip, fennel and carrot and fry for 10 minutes, stirring occasionally.

2. Pour in the stock, stir in the tomato purée and bring to the boil over a high heat. Reduce the heat, cover and simmer for 30 minutes or until the vegetables are tender.

3. Remove the lid, add the spinach, spring onions and oregano and simmer for 1–2 minutes or until the spinach has wilted. Season with salt and pepper, ladle into warm bowls and serve immediately.

TRADITIONAL ITALIAN PEASANT'S SOUP

Ribollita

This humble soup was first enjoyed by Italian peasants, who reheated minestrone or leftover vegetables and bread from the previous day and made it into a hearty meal (hence its Italian name, which translates as 'reboiled'). The soup traditionally includes cavolo nero, which is an Italian black cabbage full of flavour and goodness, but savoy cabbage or kale can be used in its place if you prefer.

SERVES 6

180g stale country-style bread
6 tablespoons olive oil
1 medium onion, peeled and
    roughly chopped
1 medium leek, thinly sliced
2 medium carrots, peeled
    and roughly chopped
2 celery sticks, roughly chopped
2 x 400g tins of borlotti beans
2 sprigs of fresh rosemary
3 sprigs of fresh thyme
2 bay leaves
1 x 400g tin of chopped tomatoes
1 tablespoon tomato purée
600ml hot vegetable stock
1 medium courgette, halved
    lengthways and roughly sliced
200g cavolo nero, tough
    central midribs removed
    and leaves shredded
Salt and white pepper

1. Preheat the oven to 180°C/gas mark 4. Put the bread on a baking sheet and bake for 10 minutes. When cool enough to handle, tear it into bite-sized chunks.

2. Heat the oil in a large, heavy-based saucepan or flameproof casserole over a medium heat. Add the onion, leek, carrots and celery and fry gently for 20 minutes, stirring occasionally.

3. Meanwhile, purée one of the tins of beans with their liquid using a blender or food processor until smooth. Rinse and drain the second tin of beans. Make a bouquet garni by binding together the rosemary, thyme and bay leaves using a little string.

4. Add the blended and drained beans, tomatoes and tomato purée to the saucepan and drop in the bouquet garni. Pour in the stock and bring to the boil over a high heat. Reduce the heat, cover and simmer gently for 45 minutes, stirring occasionally. Remove and discard the bouquet garni, add the courgette and cavolo nero and season with salt and pepper. Cover again and simmer for a further 15 minutes.

5. To serve, place a few chunks of the bread on the bottom of each warmed bowl and ladle soup over the top.

CHILLED SPICY SUMMER SOUP WITH TOMATOES, AVOCADO AND SWEETCORN

Zuppa Fredda Piccante con Pomodori, Avocado e Mais

Exquisite on a hot summer's day, this chilled vegetable soup is my take on the traditional Spanish gazpacho. It gives you such a concentrated tomato hit, and the chilli powder works really well with the sweetness of the corn. Serve with fresh, crusty bread.

SERVES 4

3 tablespoons olive oil
1/2 medium red onion, peeled
    and roughly chopped
1 x 400g tin of chopped tomatoes
1/2 teaspoon sugar
1/2 teaspoon chilli powder
600ml tomato juice
2 large fresh plum tomatoes,
    skinned, deseeded and
    cut into small cubes
1 ripe avocado, halved,
    stoned, peeled and diced
1 x 198g tin of sweetcorn kernels
2 tablespoons freshly squeezed
    lemon juice
3 tablespoons chopped
    fresh flat-leaf parsley
Salt

1. Heat the oil in a medium saucepan over a medium heat. Add the onion and fry gently for 5–10 minutes, stirring occasionally.

2. Add the tinned tomatoes, sugar and chilli powder and bring to the boil over a high heat, then reduce the heat and simmer very gently for 10 minutes covered and 10 minutes uncovered, stirring occasionally.

3. Remove the saucepan from the heat and, using a blender or food processor, blitz until smooth. Pour into a large bowl and leave to cool.

4. Add the tomato juice, fresh tomatoes, avocado, sweetcorn, lemon juice and parsley. Season with salt and stir to combine. Cover the bowl with cling film and chill in the fridge for at least 4 hours until very cold. Serve in chilled bowls.

PERFECT AUTUMN SOUP WITH BUTTERNUT SQUASH, ORANGE AND FRESH GINGER

Zuppa Autunnale con Zucca, Arance e Zenzero

I don't normally put fruit in hot savoury dishes, but the orange zest and juice in this smooth, elegant soup combines beautifully with the fresh ginger to give a lovely aromatic flavour. When buying ginger, choose fat roots as knobbly, wrinkled ones are harder to peel.

SERVES 4

3 tablespoons olive oil
1 large red onion, peeled
    and roughly chopped
3 teaspoons finely chopped
    fresh ginger
1kg butternut squash, deseeded,
    peeled and cut into 2cm chunks
1 small floury potato, such as
    Desirée or Maris Piper, peeled
    and cut into 2cm chunks
1.2 litres hot vegetable stock
3 strips orange zest
150ml freshly squeezed
    orange juice
100g mascarpone cheese
Salt and white pepper

1. Heat the oil in a medium saucepan over a medium heat. Add the onion and ginger and fry gently for 5–10 minutes, stirring occasionally.

2. Add the squash, potato and vegetable stock. Bring to the boil over a high heat then reduce the heat, cover and simmer for 25 minutes or until the squash feels tender when pierced with a knife. Add the orange zest.

3. Using a blender or food processor, blitz the soup until smooth. Pour it back into the pan, add the orange juice and season with salt and pepper. Reheat the soup until barely bubbling.

4. Ladle the soup into warm bowls and add a dollop of mascarpone on top.

SPICY PUMPKIN AND PASTA SOUP

Minestra Piccante con Zucca

Pumpkin is eaten a lot in Italy, in soups and stews, as a side dish roasted, puréed or fried, and in gnocchi and ravioli. Pumpkins come in all shapes and sizes, and we even have special festivals to celebrate these glorious vegetables! If you can't find pumpkin, use butternut squash for this recipe instead.

SERVES 4

4 tablespoons olive oil
1 medium onion, peeled
   and finely chopped
500g pumpkin, peeled, deseeded
   and cut into 1cm cubes
1/2 teaspoon chilli powder
100ml white wine
1.2 litres hot vegetable stock
150g mini pasta shapes
60g freshly grated pecorino
   cheese
Salt

1. Heat the oil in a medium saucepan over a medium heat. Add the onion and fry gently for 5 minutes, stirring occasionally. Stir in the pumpkin and chilli powder and fry for 2 minutes.

2. Increase the heat to high. Pour in the wine and cook for 2 minutes or until the liquid has evaporated, then pour in the stock and bring to the boil. Reduce the heat and simmer gently for 20 minutes, stirring occasionally.

3. Put 3 ladlesful of the soup into a bowl, making sure you have plenty of the pumpkin. Blitz until smooth using a hand-held blender then pour it back into the saucepan and season with salt.

4. Bring to a simmer, add the pasta and cook for about 5 minutes or until al dente, stirring occasionally. Remove from the heat, stir in the pecorino and serve immediately.

PEARL BARLEY, FENNEL AND CANNELLINI BEAN SOUP WITH CHEESY PANINI

Zuppa di Orzo Perlato con Finocchi, Cannellini e Panini al Formaggio

Believed to be the oldest cultivated cereal, barley is a versatile grain with a nutty texture. It's also incredibly healthy, being rich in protein and high in fibre, and is thought to lower cholesterol. For thickening and adding texture to a soup, pearl barley is ideal.

SERVES 6

4 tablespoons olive oil
1 leek, thinly sliced
1 fennel bulb, core removed
   and sliced
2 carrots, peeled and sliced
   into rounds
1 parsnip, peeled and sliced
   into half-moons
125g pearl barley, rinsed
   and drained
1.2 litres hot vegetable stock
2 tablespoons tomato purée
6 large fresh sage leaves,
   shredded
120g fine green beans,
   cut into 2cm lengths
1 x 400g tin of cannellini beans,
   rinsed and drained
Salt and freshly ground
   black pepper

For the cheesy panini
3 panini or 6 slices of white bread
3 tablespoons extra virgin olive oil
1 large garlic clove, peeled
300g Taleggio cheese, rind
   removed and cut into
   small pieces

1. Heat the olive oil in a large, heavy-based saucepan or flameproof casserole over a medium heat. Add the leek, fennel, carrots and parsnip and fry gently for 10 minutes, stirring occasionally.

2. Stir in the pearl barley then add the stock and tomato purée. Bring to the boil, add the sage and season with salt and pepper. Reduce the heat, cover and simmer gently for 40 minutes, stirring occasionally. Add the green beans and cannellini beans, re-cover and simmer for a further 20 minutes. Add a splash of boiling water if you need it.

3. Meanwhile, make the cheesy panini. Preheat the oven to 200°C/gas mark 6 and line a baking sheet with foil. Slice the panini in half lengthways and brush the cut sides with the extra virgin olive oil. Place on the lined baking sheet, cut-sides up, and bake for 15 minutes or until light brown and crispy. Remove from the oven, rub the cut sides with the garlic clove and top with the Taleggio. Return to the oven and bake for a further 3 minutes or until the cheese has melted.

4. Ladle the soup into warm bowls and serve with the cheesy panini on the side.

BIG SALADS

Many people consider salads to be healthy but dull. This probably harks back to a time when a salad meant a few wilted lettuce leaves and the odd tomato. However, while salads are indeed incredibly nutritious, they certainly do not have to be boring, as I prove in this chapter. With a vast range of fresh vegetables available throughout the year, the wonderful concoctions you can create are endless. Some are simple and best served as a side dish, while others make an exciting vegetarian starter or main course.

When making salads, always use the freshest possible ingredients; you are mainly eating vegetables raw, so they need to be full of flavour and goodness. Also, choose seasonal produce whenever possible, as it's more likely to deliver the standards you're looking for. It is also worth making the effort to dress your salads well; the dressing should complement the vegetables rather than overpowering them. Finally, please don't season and dress your salads until you're ready to serve, as doing this too early can make the ingredients turn soggy and discolour. You want all the ingredients to be at their brightest and crispiest.

Spicy Roasted Vegetable Couscous Salad

Courgette Carpaccio with Borlotti Beans,
Peppers and Capers

Fresh Mozzarella, Tomato and Basil Salad

The 'Office Lunch' Salad

Lentil, Avocado and Feta Salad

The Ultimate Italian Bread and Tomato Salad

Fruity, Mixed-grain Salad with Avocado,
Rocket and Fresh Mint

Warm Honeyed Parsnip, Carrot and Beetroot
Salad with Horseradish Dressing

Chargrilled Little Gem Lettuce,
Chicory and Pea Salad

New Potato, Tenderstem Broccoli and
Hazelnut Salad with Gorgonzola

SPICY ROASTED VEGETABLE COUSCOUS SALAD

Insalata di Couscous con Verdure Piccanti al Forno

Couscous is so versatile as it absorbs any flavours you add to it. The tomatoes in this recipe 'pop' as they cook, releasing all their lovely syrupy juices – and when stirred into the couscous they, along with the other vegetables, transform the bland grain into something really delicious.

SERVES 4

1 red pepper, deseeded and
   cut into 2cm chunks
1 yellow pepper, deseeded
   and cut into 2cm chunks
2 courgettes, cut into 2cm chunks
1 aubergine, cut into 2cm chunks
2 small red onions, peeled and
   cut into 6 wedges
150g fresh red cherry tomatoes
100g fresh yellow cherry tomatoes
1 teaspoon dried chilli flakes
8 tablespoons olive oil
250g couscous
1 pinch of sweet smoked paprika
Handful (about 40g) of small
   basil leaves
Balsamic glaze for drizzling
Salt to taste

1. Preheat the oven to 180°C/gas mark 4. Place the peppers, courgettes, aubergine and onions in a large, shallow roasting tin. Add the tomatoes and chilli flakes, drizzle over 5 tablespoons of the oil and season well with salt. Toss everything together so all the vegetables are well coated in the oil. Roast for 45 minutes, stirring or shaking the vegetables every 10 minutes.

2. Meanwhile, place the couscous in a large heatproof bowl. Add the paprika with a good pinch of salt and stir to combine. Pour over just enough boiling water to cover the couscous, cover with cling film and leave for about 10 minutes or until all the water is absorbed. Fluff up the grains with a fork and check the seasoning, then pour in the remaining oil and stir gently to combine.

3. Tip the roasted vegetables into the bowl with the couscous. Add a splash of warm water to the empty roasting tin, stir to combine with the flavoursome juices in the tin, then pour the liquid over the couscous and vegetables. Gently mix all the ingredients together and fold in the basil.

4. Check for seasoning one more time and transfer to a serving platter. Serve warm or at room temperature drizzled with a little balsamic glaze.

COURGETTE CARPACCIO WITH BORLOTTI BEANS, PEPPERS AND CAPERS

Carpaccio di Zucchine con Borlotti, Peperoni e Capperi

This is a great vegetarian alternative to raw meat or fish carpaccio. The marinating of the thinly sliced courgettes makes them so soft they don't need any cooking. If using small, young courgettes you can use the whole vegetable, but for larger courgettes I suggest you use the flesh only, as the seeds can be spongy when eaten raw. Just halve the courgettes lengthways, run a teaspoon down the centre of each half, and scoop out and discard the seeds. Serve with toasted ciabatta.

SERVES 4

4 small, young courgettes
Grated zest and juice of 1 lemon
4 tablespoons extra virgin olive oil
1 x 400g tin of borlotti beans,
    rinsed and drained
1 small yellow pepper, deseeded
    and finely diced
1 tablespoon baby capers, drained
1 tablespoon chopped fresh
    flat-leaf parsley
Small fresh basil leaves to garnish
Parmesan cheese shavings to serve
Salt and freshly ground
    black pepper

1. Using a vegetable peeler or mandolin held over a large bowl, shave the courgettes lengthways into long, thin strips. Add the lemon zest and juice and 2 tablespoons of the oil and season with a little salt and black pepper. Gently toss everything together with your hands. Leave to rest for 10 minutes to allow the courgettes to soften.

2. Meanwhile, place the beans and yellow pepper in a medium bowl. Add the remaining oil, the capers and the parsley and season with salt and pepper. Toss together to combine.

3. To serve, lay the courgette strips on 4 plates, slightly overlapping. Spoon over the borlotti and pepper mixture then scatter over the basil leaves and Parmesan shavings.

FRESH MOZZARELLA, TOMATO AND BASIL SALAD

Insalata Caprese

Tomato and mozzarella salad is generally eaten at least once a week in Italian households. Beautifully simple, the key to its success is to use top-quality ingredients. Select perfectly ripe tomatoes that smell of summer and store them at room temperature rather than in the fridge; if eaten cold, they lack flavour.

SERVES 4

600g mixed varieties of fresh
   tomatoes (including cherry
   tomatoes, medium-sized
   varieties and beef tomatoes)
50g sun-dried tomatoes
   in oil, drained
1 small garlic clove
2 x 125g balls of buffalo mozzarella
   cheese, drained and torn into
   bite-sized pieces
60g salad leaves (e.g. rocket,
   watercress, baby spinach)
3 tablespoons extra virgin olive oil
Small handful (about 25g) of fresh
   basil leaves, shredded
Salt and freshly ground
   black pepper

1. Halve the cherry tomatoes, quarter the medium-sized varieties and slice the larger beef tomatoes. Place them all in a large bowl.

2. Finely chop the sun-dried tomatoes and garlic together and add to the bowl with the fresh tomatoes. Scatter over the mozzarella and add the salad leaves. Drizzle over the oil and season well with salt and pepper.

3. Lightly toss all the ingredients together. Arrange the tomatoes on a serving platter, scatter over the shredded basil and serve.

THE 'OFFICE LUNCH' SALAD

Insalata per l'Ufficio

This is the perfect salad to take to work. In the morning, arrange all the ingredients in an airtight container in the order specified, then at lunchtime simply shake the box so all the ingredients are combined. The vegetables will stay crunchy and fresh, rather than turning soggy as salads that are prepared ahead often do. This recipe makes enough for two salads, so you will need two containers – one for you and one for your partner – or keep the second salad in the fridge for the following day.

SERVES 2

1 red pepper, deseeded and
 finely diced
1 x 400g tin of chickpeas,
 rinsed and drained
50g frozen or tinned
 sweetcorn kernels
6cm piece of cucumber, diced
12 pitted black olives,
 drained and halved
2 large handfuls of crispy
 salad leaves
Salt and freshly ground
 black pepper

For the dressing
5 tablespoons mayonnaise
Juice of 1/2 lemon
2 tablespoons extra virgin olive oil
1 small garlic clove, grated
30g Gorgonzola, crumbled

1. First, make the dressing. Put the mayonnaise in a medium bowl and add the lemon juice, oil and a little of the garlic to taste. Whisk together. Add a splash of water and whisk again to create a thick pouring consistency. Fold in the Gorgonzola. Season with some salt and pepper.

2. Divide the dressing between 2 plastic airtight containers and shake them slightly to spread the mixture over the bottom. (The containers need to be large enough to hold all the ingredients plus have a little extra space at the top to allow them to move freely when shaken.)

3. In each container lay the vegetables on top of the dressing in the following order: pepper, chickpeas, sweetcorn (it doesn't matter if the kernels are still frozen as they will have defrosted by lunch time), cucumber, olives and, finally, the salad leaves. Add a little black pepper, cover and seal tightly. When ready to eat, simply shake everything together.

LENTIL, AVOCADO AND FETA SALAD

Insalata di Lenticchie, Avocado e Feta

Tinned beans have long been a storecupboard staple in my house, but cooked lentils, in tins or packets, are relatively recent and I am never without. They are so easy and convenient, and are perfect for making quick, nutritious salads such as this one. Make sure you drain the lentils well and leave them to dry before making the salad. Serve with warm, crusty bread.

SERVES 4

1 large red onion, peeled
   and finely sliced
Juice of 1 orange
1 x 400g tin of Puy lentils,
   rinsed and drained
1/2 cucumber, halved lengthways,
   deseeded and sliced
1 ripe avocado, halved,
   stoned, peeled and diced
70g rocket leaves
100g feta cheese
20 small mint leaves

For the dressing
1 teaspoon Dijon mustard
1 teaspoon runny honey
2 tablespoons balsamic vinegar
4 tablespoons extra virgin olive oil
Salt and freshly ground
   black pepper

1. Place the onion in a small bowl and pour over the orange juice. Leave to marinate for 10 minutes.

2. Meanwhile, tip the lentils into a large bowl and add the cucumber. Drain the onion, discarding the orange juice, and add to the bowl with the lentils.

3. To make the dressing, combine the mustard, honey and vinegar in a small bowl. Whisk in the oil gradually, mix in 1 tablespoon of water and season with salt and pepper.

4. Just before serving, pour the dressing over the lentils and add the avocado and rocket leaves. Gently toss everything together and transfer to a large serving platter. Crumble over the feta and sprinkle with the mint leaves. Serve immediately.

THE ULTIMATE ITALIAN BREAD AND TOMATO SALAD

Panzanella

The key ingredients of panzanella, a popular Tuscan salad, are fresh ripe tomatoes and leftover bread dressed with olive oil and vinegar. Other vegetables are usually added, but these can vary, so although I'm providing a list of ingredients here, don't worry about following it precisely – experiment using whatever vegetables you have to hand in your fridge. It is best made in summer, when tomatoes are at their best. Serve with a glass of Italian red wine.

SERVES 4

6 thick slices of stale country-style
    bread, cut into 2cm cubes
6 fresh ripe tomatoes,
    roughly chopped
12 semi-dried tomatoes
    in oil, drained
280g chargrilled red peppers
    in a jar, drained and
    roughly chopped
2 tablespoons capers, drained
1 medium red onion, peeled
    and finely sliced
2 celery sticks, finely chopped
6 tablespoons extra virgin olive oil
2 tablespoons white wine vinegar
Small handful (about 25g) of fresh
    basil leaves, torn
Salt and freshly ground
    black pepper

1. Preheat the oven to 190°C/gas mark 5. Arrange the bread on a large baking sheet in a single layer and toast in the oven for 5 minutes until crispy on the outside but still soft in the middle.

2. Place the toasted bread in a large bowl. Drizzle over 3 tablespoons of cold water until moistened but not soggy. Add the fresh and semi-dried tomatoes, red peppers, capers, onion, celery, oil and vinegar, and season with some salt and pepper.

3. Lightly toss everything together until all the ingredients are well combined. Add the basil, toss once more and serve straightaway.

FRUITY, MIXED-GRAIN SALAD WITH AVOCADO, ROCKET AND FRESH MINT

Insalata Fruttata di Cereali Misti con Avocado, Rucola e Menta

Grains all require different cooking times, so making a mixed-grain salad can be a bit of a faff if you prepare it from scratch. Thankfully, you can now buy cooked mixed grains that taste delicious as well as being very wholesome. The mixtures generally include wheat, bulgur wheat, red quinoa, red lentils and toasted soya flakes. Serve the salad straightaway, so the avocado doesn't discolour.

SERVES 4

2 x 250g packets of ready-
   to-eat mixed grains
40g dried cranberries
50g ready-to-eat dried apricots,
   roughly chopped
3 spring onions, finely chopped
1 ripe avocado, halved, stoned,
   peeled and diced
Juice of 1 lemon
3 tablespoons extra virgin
   olive oil
8 fresh mint leaves,
   finely shredded
2 large handfuls of rocket leaves
200ml plain yogurt
1 tablespoon white wine vinegar
Salt and freshly ground
   black pepper

1. Tip the mixed grains into a large bowl. Stir in the cranberries, apricots, spring onions and avocado. Pour over the lemon juice and 1 tablespoon of the oil, season with salt and pepper and mix in the mint.

2. Transfer the salad to a serving platter. Scatter over the rocket and drizzle over another 1 tablespoon of the oil.

3. Put the yogurt, vinegar and the remaining 1 tablespoon of oil into a small bowl, stir to combine and season with salt and pepper. Spoon over a little of the yogurt mixture and serve the rest on the side.

WARM HONEYED PARSNIP, CARROT AND BEETROOT SALAD WITH HORSERADISH DRESSING

Insalata Invernale di Pastinaca al Miele, Carote e Rape Rosse con Condimento al Rafano

Salads don't have to be cold; warm salads in autumn and winter are a real treat, and you can take advantage of the delicious variety of seasonal root vegetables available. I frequently make this as a first course for my family – it looks so colourful, and I love the combination of the warm and cool elements.

SERVES 4

2 large carrots, peeled and cut
  lengthways into thin slices
2 medium parsnips, peeled and
  cut lengthways into thin slices
3 tablespoons olive oil
2 sprigs of fresh rosemary
2 tablespoons runny honey
3 small cooked beetroot (room
  temperature), quartered
Handful of mixed leaves (rocket,
  watercress, baby spinach)

For the dressing
3 tablespoons crème fraîche
1 tablespoon creamed horseradish
Juice of 1/2 lemon
Salt and freshly ground
  black pepper

1. Bring a medium saucepan of salted water to the boil. Add the carrots and parsnips, bring back to the boil and cook for 2 minutes. Tip into a colander set over the sink then rinse immediately under cold running water.

2. To make the dressing, mix together the crème fraîche, horseradish and lemon juice, and season with salt and pepper. Set aside.

3. Heat the oil in a large frying pan over a high heat. Add the carrots and parsnips, then the rosemary and the honey. Stir to combine and season with a little salt and pepper. After about 1 minute, when the honey has thickened and is coating the vegetables well, remove from the heat and discard the rosemary.

4. Divide the vegetables between 4 serving plates. Top with the beetroot wedges and mixed leaves. Serve warm, with a tablespoonful of the dressing on the side and the pan juices drizzled over.

CHARGRILLED LITTLE GEM LETTUCE, CHICORY AND PEA SALAD

Insalata di Cuori di Lattuga e Cicoria Grigliati e Piselli

Little Gem lettuces and chicory are both delicious chargrilled; they retain their texture after cooking and complement each other perfectly, with the sweetness of the lettuce offsetting the bitterness of the chicory. Ricotta salata is much firmer and saltier than regular ricotta. If you can't find it, use goat's cheese instead.

SERVES 4

4 heads of Little Gem lettuce, quartered lengthways
4 heads of chicory (white/green or red), halved lengthways
2 tablespoons olive oil for brushing and frying
2 Italian flatbreads or tortilla wraps, torn into bite-sized pieces
100g frozen peas, defrosted
150g ricotta salata
Salt and freshly ground black pepper

For the dressing
1 teaspoon Dijon mustard
2 tablespoons red wine vinegar
1 tablespoon chopped fresh tarragon
1 shallot, peeled and finely chopped
5 tablespoons extra virgin olive oil

1. Preheat a ridged cast-iron chargrill pan and a medium frying pan over a high heat. Brush the cut sides of the lettuce and chicory pieces with 1 tablespoon of the olive oil. Set aside.

2. Make the dressing by whisking together the mustard and vinegar, then add the tarragon and shallot. Gradually whisk in the extra virgin olive oil, followed by a splash of water, and season with salt and pepper. Set aside.

3. Heat the remaining tablespoon of the olive oil in the frying pan over a high heat. Fry the flatbreads for 1 minute each side or until golden brown and crispy, then season with salt. Transfer to kitchen paper to drain.

4. Meanwhile, place the lettuce and chicory in the chargrill pan in a single layer, oiled-side down, and cook for 1 minute on each side or until lightly charred and slightly softened, then transfer to a large bowl. You will need to do this in batches. Add the peas and stir in enough dressing to coat all the ingredients evenly.

5. Place the lettuce and chicory on a large serving platter, crumble over the ricotta salata and scatter with the crispy flatbread. Drizzle over a little extra dressing.

NEW POTATO, TENDERSTEM BROCCOLI AND HAZELNUT SALAD WITH GORGONZOLA

Insalata di Patate Novelle con Broccoli, Nocciole e Gorgonzola

Potato salad is a classic dish, but all too often the potatoes are covered in a thick, creamy dressing which can be a bit too heavy. This recipe is much lighter and comes with warm broccoli and roasted hazelnuts for a bit of added crunch and vitamin boost, and – just because I love it – a bit of oozy, creamy Gorgonzola.

SERVES 4

400g baby new potatoes, scrubbed and larger ones cut in half
300g Tenderstem broccoli
1 teaspoon Dijon mustard
2 tablespoons white wine vinegar
2 tablespoons hazelnut oil
2 tablespoons extra virgin olive oil
75g roasted skinned hazelnuts, lightly crushed
150g Gorgonzola cheese (chilled)
1 tablespoon chopped fresh chives
Salt and freshly ground black pepper

1. Put the potatoes in a large pan of boiling, salted water, bring back to the boil and simmer for about 10–12 minutes or until just tender. Add the broccoli and cook for a further 1–2 minutes.

2. Tip the vegetables into a colander set over the sink and rinse for 1 minute under cold running water. Leave to drain.

3. Meanwhile, put the mustard and vinegar in a large bowl. Gradually whisk in both the oils and season well with salt and pepper. Add the warm potatoes and broccoli and mix gently until evenly coated with the dressing. Transfer to a large serving platter.

4. Scatter the hazelnuts, Gorgonzola and chives over the top. Gently mix together and serve warm.

SIDES
and accompaniments

When planning a meal, we often tend to focus on the main dish, with the accompaniments being a bit of an afterthought. However, I find that carefully chosen side dishes really enhance the meal and can be every bit as good as the dish taking centre stage.

In Italy we usually serve pasta as a starter, so we don't generally serve carbs – such as potatoes or rice – with our main meal. However, in this chapter I have opted to include the potato due to its versatility and popularity. Another difference between our cultures is that Italians tend to serve accompaniments on separate plates, allowing each side dish to retain its own flavour and texture rather than absorbing the juices or sauces of the main course. I still tend to serve them this way, and when having a dinner party I really do feel it looks more impressive – give it a go!

Baby Courgettes Marinated in Garlic
and Herb Vinaigrette

Spinach and Chickpeas with Chilli and Garlic

Lentils and Artichokes with Salsa Verde

Aubergine and Courgette Gratin with Mozzarella

Roast Potatoes and Aubergines
with Garlic and Lemon

Potato, Parsnip and Mustard Gratin
with Thyme

Double-baked Jacket Potatoes with
Creamy Leeks and Gorgonzola

Mashed Sweet Potatoes with
Garlic Butter and Mascarpone

BABY COURGETTES MARINATED IN GARLIC AND HERB VINAIGRETTE

Zucchine Marinate con Vinaigrette all' Aglio ed Erbe

These baby courgettes are cooked for a very short time, because the marinating process will continue to soften them as well as adding flavour. Make these in summer, when courgettes are small, tender and very flavoursome. Serve with grilled fish or chicken.

SERVES 4

400g baby courgettes,
    quartered lengthways
1 teaspoon wholegrain mustard
1 tablespoon runny honey
2 tablespoons white wine vinegar
1 garlic clove, peeled and crushed
6 tablespoons extra virgin olive oil
3 tablespoons chopped fresh
    flat-leaf parsley
3 tablespoons chopped
    fresh oregano
3 tablespoons chopped
    fresh tarragon
Salt and freshly ground
    black pepper

1. Put the courgettes in a medium pan of boiling, salted water, bring back to the boil and simmer for 2 minutes. Drain thoroughly and tip into a large serving dish to cool slightly.

2. Meanwhile, to prepare the dressing combine the mustard, honey, vinegar and garlic in a small bowl. Whisk in the oil gradually, mix in 1 tablespoon of water and add the herbs.

3. Pour the dressing over the warm courgettes and gently turn to coat. Cover with cling film and place in the fridge for 4–6 hours to marinate, turning once or twice.

4. About half an hour before serving, remove from the fridge and just before serving season with salt and pepper.

SPINACH AND CHICKPEAS WITH CHILLI AND GARLIC

Spinaci e Ceci all' Aglio e Peperoncino

In southern Italy, especially Sicily, you can see a strong North African influence in the food, for instance in the use of couscous and, as in this recipe, chickpeas. The combination of fried spinach, chickpeas, garlic and chilli makes a perfect side dish served with chicken, veal or pork alla Milanese. If you're vegetarian, serve a poached egg on top of the spinach for a delicious and nutritious meal.

SERVES 4

4 tablespoons extra virgin
    olive oil
2 garlic cloves, crushed
1/2 teaspoon dried chilli flakes
400g fresh spinach
1 x 400g tin of chickpeas, drained
30g unsalted butter
Salt

1. Heat the oil in a large saucepan over a medium heat. Add the garlic and chilli flakes and fry for 30 seconds, stirring constantly.

2. Add the spinach to the pan in stages, stirring and waiting for each batch to wilt before adding another handful. This will take about 5 minutes.

3. Stir in the chickpeas and butter and cook for 3 minutes or until the chickpeas are heated through. Season with salt and serve.

LENTILS AND ARTICHOKES WITH SALSA VERDE

Lenticchie e Carciofi in Salsa Verde

Lentils are so nutritious and full of fibre, but they can also be a little drab. Combining them with salsa verde and artichoke hearts really perks them up, giving them a chance to show how great they can really be. Serve this dish with white fish or a stew.

SERVES 4

1 x 400g tin of brown lentils,
   rinsed and drained
100g artichoke hearts in oil,
   drained and roughly chopped
50g sun-dried tomatoes in oil,
   drained and finely chopped
2 fresh plum tomatoes,
   roughly chopped
100g pecorino cheese, roughly
   chopped into small pieces
Salt and freshly ground
   black pepper

For the salsa verde
1 garlic clove, peeled and crushed
1 teaspoon wholegrain mustard
50g rocket leaves
10g fresh flat-leaf parsley
1 tablespoon balsamic vinegar
8 tablespoons extra virgin
   olive oil
20g toasted pine nuts
1 tablespoon freshly squeezed
   lemon juice

1. Place all the ingredients for the salsa verde in a food processor and blitz until smooth.

2. Tip the lentils into a medium bowl. Pour three-quarters of the salsa verde over the lentils and stir to combine. Add the artichokes, sun-dried tomatoes, fresh tomatoes and pecorino. Season with salt and pepper and gently toss everything together.

3. Pile into a serving bowl and drizzle over the remaining salsa verde.

AUBERGINE AND COURGETTE GRATIN WITH MOZZARELLA

Gratinato di Melanzane e Zucchine con Mozzarella

I love the taste of ratatouille, but it can become monotonous, particularly if you eat it frequently, so I came up with the idea of a ratatouille gratin, adding mozzarella and Parmesan cheese to give the dish a bit more oomph. Serve with grilled meats.

SERVES 6

3 courgettes, about 250g in total
6 tablespoons olive oil
2 onions, peeled and finely
   chopped
2 celery sticks, roughly chopped
1 red pepper, deseeded and
   cut into 1cm cubes
6 tablespoons fresh oregano leaves
2 aubergines, about 750g in total,
   cut into 1cm cubes
1 x 400g tin of chopped tomatoes
25g toasted pine nuts
2 tablespoons balsamic vinegar
15 fresh basil leaves, shredded
80g freshly grated Parmesan
   cheese
2 x 125g balls of mozzarella
   cheese, drained and cut
   into small chunks
2 tablespoons extra virgin
   olive oil
Salt and freshly ground
   black pepper

1. Preheat the oven to 180°C/gas mark 4. Use a vegetable peeler or mandolin to shave the courgettes lengthways into long, thin strips. Set aside.

2. Heat 3 tablespoons of the olive oil in a large, heavy-based frying pan over a medium heat. Add the onions, celery, red pepper and oregano and fry gently for 7 minutes, stirring occasionally.

3. Increase the heat to medium high. Add the remaining olive oil and the aubergines and cook for 7 minutes, stirring from time to time. Tip in the tomatoes and add the pine nuts and vinegar. Bring to the boil then simmer for 5 minutes. Stir in the basil and half the Parmesan, season with salt and pepper and stir to combine.

4. Tip the mixture into a baking dish measuring about 20 x 30cm. Dot the mozzarella evenly over the aubergine mixture and lay the courgettes on top. Sprinkle over the remaining Parmesan, drizzle over the extra virgin olive oil and season with black pepper. Bake for 20 minutes. Serve piping hot.

ROAST POTATOES AND AUBERGINES WITH GARLIC AND LEMON

Patate e Melanzane al Forno con Aglio e Limone

Roast potatoes and aubergines make perfect partners, and both are good combined with garlic, lemon and herbs as in this recipe. Make sure you use a large enough roasting tin so the vegetables can spread out and become golden and crispy. Serve with any grilled or pan-fried fish.

SERVES 6

600g Maris Piper potatoes,
   peeled and cut into 3cm chunks
10 tablespoons vegetable oil
2 aubergines, about 250g each,
   cut into 2cm cubes
3 garlic cloves, peeled and sliced
4 tablespoons chopped fresh
   flat-leaf parsley
Grated zest and juice
   of 1 unwaxed lemon
Salt and freshly ground
   black pepper

1. Preheat the oven to 190°C/gas mark 5. Put the potatoes in a large pan, cover with cold, salted water and bring to the boil over a high heat. Boil rapidly for 2 minutes. Drain and return to the pan and place over a medium heat for 2 minutes to dry out. Cover and then shake the potatoes to fluff up the edges.

2. Meanwhile, pour the oil into a large roasting tin and place in the preheated oven for 10 minutes or until the oil is sizzling hot.

3. Carefully put the potatoes into the hot oil. Season with plenty of salt and pepper and turn the potatoes to coat them in the oil. Roast for 45 minutes, turning after 20 minutes and scraping the bits that are stuck to the bottom of the tin.

4. Lift out the tin and add the aubergines and garlic. Add a little more salt and turn the vegetables so they are well coated in the oil. Return the tin to the oven for 45 minutes, stirring halfway through.

5. Transfer the vegetables to a serving dish and sprinkle over the chopped parsley and lemon zest and juice. Serve immediately.

POTATO, PARSNIP AND MUSTARD GRATIN WITH THYME

Gratinato di Patate e Pastinaca con Senape e Timo

Parsnips have a unique, intensely sweet flavour, yet there are surprisingly few side dishes that contain them. This gratin is easy to make and never fails to impress. While you're preparing the potatoes and parsnips, place them in a bowl of cold water to prevent them from discolouring, and drain and dry thoroughly before you cook with them. Serve with almost any meat and fish, or with a salad.

SERVES 6

2 tablespoons olive oil
50g salted butter
2 garlic cloves, peeled and crushed
2 tablespoons Dijon mustard
2 tablespoons lemon juice
3 tablespoons fresh thyme leaves
4 waxy potatoes, peeled and
  thinly sliced
2 medium parsnips, peeled
  and thinly sliced
100ml hot vegetable stock
Salt and freshly ground
  black pepper

1. Preheat the oven to 180°C/gas mark 4. Heat the oil and butter in a flameproof casserole. Add the garlic and fry gently for about 30 seconds, stirring. As soon as the garlic starts to sizzle, stir in the mustard, lemon juice and half the thyme. Transfer the mixture to a small bowl.

2. Layer one-third of the potatoes and parsnips in the casserole. Spoon over one-third of the garlic, mustard and thyme mixture and season well. Repeat the process twice then sprinkle over the reserved thyme. Pour the stock down the sides of the casserole to prevent washing away the seasoning on the top.

3. Cover the casserole with greaseproof paper and then the lid to stop the potatoes from burning. Bake for 1 hour. Remove the paper and lid and continue to bake for a further 20 minutes or until the gratin is golden brown and crispy on top.

DOUBLE-BAKED JACKET POTATOES WITH CREAMY LEEKS AND GORGONZOLA

Patate Intere con Buccia Cotte al Forno con Porri Cremosi e Gorgonzola

Jacket potatoes are the ultimate comfort food, particularly when combined with these creamy, cheesy leeks. I've used Gorgonzola dolce, which is sweeter and softer than Gorgonzola piccante, and better for cooking as it melts so beautifully. Serve with roasted vegetables.

SERVES 4

2 large baking potatoes
25g salted butter
1 large leek, halved and
    thinly sliced
100g mascarpone cheese
100g Gorgonzola dolce cheese,
    broken into small pieces
Freshly ground black pepper

1. Preheat the oven to 200°C/gas mark 6. Prick the potatoes with a fork several times. Bake for 1½ hours, turning halfway through, or until the centre feels soft when a knife is inserted.

2. Meanwhile, melt the butter in a small pan over a medium heat. Add the leek and fry for 10 minutes until tender, stirring occasionally. Remove from the heat.

3. When the potatoes are cool enough to handle, halve them and scoop out the middle, leaving a thin shell. Add the potato flesh to the leeks together with the mascarpone. Mash using a fork or potato masher then stir in the Gorgonzola.

4. Pile the cheesy potato mixture back into the potato skins and bake for a further 20 minutes. Finish with a few grindings of black pepper.

MASHED SWEET POTATOES WITH GARLIC BUTTER AND MASCARPONE

Puré di Patate Dolci con Burro all' Aglio e Mascarpone

Despite their name, sweet potatoes are actually a root vegetable rather than a type of potato. They have sweet-tasting, pale yellow or orange flesh and a lovely creamy texture, and are a rich source of vitamins, minerals and fibre. When they're mashed with mascarpone, garlic butter and parsley they make a fluffy, super-indulgent side dish to accompany ham or a salad.

SERVES 4-6

4–5 sweet potatoes, 1kg in total,
   peeled and sliced into rounds
   1cm thick
50g salted butter
3 garlic cloves, peeled and crushed
100g mascarpone cheese
3 tablespoons roughly chopped
   fresh flat-leaf parsley
Salt and white pepper

1. Preheat the oven to 180°C/gas mark 4. Place the sweet potatoes in a large pan, cover with cold, salted water and bring to the boil over a high heat. Reduce the heat and simmer gently for 15 minutes or until tender.

2. Meanwhile, make the garlic butter. Melt the butter in a small saucepan over a very low heat. Add the garlic and fry gently for 2 minutes, stirring constantly, then remove from the heat. Make sure you do not burn the garlic or it will taste bitter.

3. Drain the sweet potatoes, tip them back into the pan and purée using a hand-held blender or mash using a potato masher or ricer until very smooth. Add the garlic butter and blitz for 10 seconds, then the mascarpone and parsley and blitz again for about 10 seconds or until smooth and creamy. Season with salt and pepper.

4. Spoon the mashed sweet potato into a baking dish and cover with foil. Bake for 15 minutes or until piping hot. Serve immediately.

INDEX

First published in Great Britain in 2015 by Hodder & Stoughton
An Hachette UK company

1

Copyright © Gino D'Acampo 2015

Photography Copyright © David Munns 2015

The right of Gino D'Acampo to be identified as the Author of the
Work has been asserted by him in accordance with the Copyright,
Designs and Patents Act 1988.

A CIP catalogue record for this title is available from the
British Library

Hardback ISBN 978 1 444 79519 6
Ebook ISBN 978 1 444 79520 2

Editorial Director: Nicky Ross
Editor: Sarah Hammond
Project Editor: Polly Boyd
Design & Art Direction: Smith & Gilmour
Photographer: David Munns
Props Stylist: Victoria Allen
Food Stylist: Gee Charman

Typeset in Sentinel, Lulo and Lobster by Smith & Gilmour

Printed and bound in Germany by Mohn Media

Hodder & Stoughton policy is to use papers that are natural,
renewable and recyclable products and made from wood grown
in sustainable forests. The logging and manufacturing processes
are expected to conform to the environmental regulations
of the country of origin.

Hodder & Stoughton Ltd
Carmelite House
50 Victoria Embankment
London EC4Y 0DZ

www.hodder.co.uk

Acknowledgements

As I reached my thirteenth book, I was expecting
some acknowledgements to change as different
people have helped, inspired and supported me
over the years – but I find they remain pretty much
the same as for my first book. I feel extremely lucky
to still have you all in my life and please know that
my thanks really do come from my heart.

Once again a big thank you to all the crew at Hodder
& Stoughton, who trusted me with writing another
cookbook for them. Fantastic working with you
guys – let's keep doing it!

To everybody at Bonta Italia, especially my best
friend and business partner, Marco Silvagni. Grazie
for supporting me in every way!

A big kiss to Abbie, who always helps me look a lot
less baggy-eyed with her great make-up skills!

Lots of love to the team at My Pasta Bar and, of course,
to all at Jeremy Hicks Associates. An extra big snog
to Charlotte for all you do and, as always, lots of love,
admiration and respect for father-figure and agent
'Don', Mr Jeremy Hicks.

To my favourite girls, Ali Shalson & Gee Charman;
thank you for your culinary skills and for helping me
to make sure all my recipes are perfectly executed!

Last but not least to my wonderful family: Jessie –
you are everything in my world that makes sense.
Luci & Rocco – I am so incredibly proud of you both
and so lucky to be your daddy. Mia – you are daddy's
little princess and have me completely wrapped
around your little finger – I love it!

Finally, thank you all for continuing to buy my books,
watch my shows and generally support me. It really
does mean everything to me and makes it all
worthwhile!

www.ginodacampo.com